IL PRIMO LIBRO
DE MADRIGALI
A SEI VOCI

RECENT RESEARCHES IN THE MUSIC OF THE RENAISSANCE

James Haar, general editor

A-R Editions, Inc., publishes six quarterly series—

Recent Researches in the Music of the Middle Ages and Early Renaissance
Margaret Bent, general editor

Recent Researches in the Music of the Renaissance
James Haar, general editor

Recent Researches in the Music of the Baroque Era
Robert L. Marshall, general editor

Recent Researches in the Music of the Classical Era
Eugene K. Wolf, general editor

Recent Researches in the Music of the Nineteenth and Early Twentieth Centuries
Rufus Hallmark, general editor

Recent Researches in American Music
H. Wiley Hitchcock, general editor—

which make public music that is being brought to light
in the course of current musicological research.

Each volume in the *Recent Researches* is devoted
to works by a single composer or to a single genre of composition,
chosen because of its potential interest to scholars and performers,
and prepared for publication according to the standards that govern
the making of all reliable historical editions.

Correspondence should be addressed:

A-R EDITIONS, INC.
315 West Gorham Street
Madison, Wisconsin 53703

RECENT RESEARCHES IN THE MUSIC OF THE RENAISSANCE • VOLUMES LXX and LXXI

Alessandro Striggio

IL PRIMO LIBRO
DE MADRIGALI
A SEI VOCI

Edited by David S. Butchart

A-R EDITIONS, INC. • MADISON

For my parents

Library of Congress Cataloging in Publication Data

Striggio, Alessandro, 1536 or 7–1592.
    [Madrigals, voices (6), book 1]
    Il primo libro de madrigali a sei voci.

    (Recent researches in the music of the Renaissance,
0486–123X ; v. 70–71)
    For mixed voices.
    Edited principally from the 1565 ed. (Venice :
A. Gardano) in the Civico museo bibliografico musicale,
Bologna; includes 3 madrigals added for the 1565 ed.
    Texts, with English translations and critical
commentary: p.
    Includes bibliographical notes.
    Partial contents: Madrigali aggiunti. Rosa eterna,
immortal sacro giacinto / Alessandro Striggio.
L'alma mia fiamma, oltra le belle bella / Claudio
Merulo. Anchor che col partire / Perissone Cambio.
    1. Madrigals (Music), Italian.   I. Butchart, David S.
II. Title.   III. Series.
M2.R2384   vol. 70-71   [1582]   86–750095
ISBN 0–89579–206–0

Contents

Preface

Alessandro Striggio was one of the leading Italian composers in the second half of the sixteenth century and certainly the greatest musician active in Florence between 1560 and 1590. The attention attracted by some aspects of his career—his vital role in Medici festivities, his cultivation of the so-called "madrigal comedy"—has overshadowed interest in what is the most substantial part of his musical legacy, his serious madrigal production.[1] The present edition of Striggio's *Primo libro de madrigali a sei voci* seeks to remedy that situation in part by making available the composer's most renowned collection of madrigals, one that contains some of his most famous and considered settings.[2]

Alessandro Striggio

Born in Mantua in 1536 or 1537 into a well-established noble family of the city,[3] Striggio was the illegitimate son of a celebrated Mantuan soldier (also called Alessandro), who had had only daughters by his marriage. For this reason, perhaps, the young Alessandro was made his father's universal heir in the latter's will, signed in 1547.[4] Little is known about the composer's early life and musical training. The suggestion, made by Alfred Einstein, that Giaches de Wert may have been his teacher can almost certainly be discounted.[5] Although Striggio was without doubt musically active in his native city and at the court of the duke of Mantua during the 1550s, the first firm date in his career is 1 March 1559, when he entered the service of Cosimo I de' Medici, duke of Florence, at a salary of 21 *scudi*, 3 *lire* a month.[6] In the relevant *Nota de salariati* he was called simply *musico*; but as he was the highest-paid of any of the ten musicians mentioned, this may already indicate a certain reputation, a suggestion backed up by two references in near-contemporary literary works.[7] Striggio played a variety of musical instruments, including the viol, the lute, and the *lira da braccio*; he was particularly renowned as a virtuoso on the *lirone* or *lira grande*, a large version of the *lira da braccio*.[8]

Less than a year after taking up his post, Striggio asked permission of his master to go to Venice to publish some of his music.[9] In all probability he saw both his *Primo libro de madrigali a cinque voci* and his *Primo libro de madrigali a sei voci* through the presses. He sent copies of each to Guglielmo Gonzaga, the duke of Mantua and Striggio's former patron, on 1 June 1560.[10]

Within the same year, each book had been reprinted, the five-voice collection twice. For Striggio it was the beginning of an illustrious career. Tangible signs of his valuable service at court came in succeeding years, when he composed the greater part of the festive music for three Medici celebrations: the festivities connected with the wedding of the prince regent, Francesco (1565/66); the baptism of Francesco's daughter Eleonora (1568); and the visit to Florence of Archduke Karl of Austria (1569).[11] In the same period, Striggio's musical horizons were broadening. In 1567 he undertook a journey through Europe, visiting the imperial courts at Vienna and Brno, the Bavarian courts at Munich and Augsburg, the court of the French king at Paris, and finally that of Elizabeth I of England.[12] He entertained the royal personages with his instrumental performances and with his madrigals, and in Munich and Paris he had a forty-part mass of his performed. Well received wherever he went, he was also made tempting offers of employment. The following year (1568) Striggio formed part of the Medici entourage in Munich at the wedding of Duke Wilhelm of Bavaria and Renée of Lorraine.[13] During this decade, he had continued to publish new compositions in several madrigal anthologies. His main efforts, however, went into three "madrigal comedies," *Il cicalamento delle donne al bucato* and *La caccia*, in 1567, and *Il gioco di primiera*, in 1569. In 1570 and 1571, Striggio brought out two more collections of madrigals, *Il secondo libro de madrigali a cinque voci* and *Il secondo libro de madrigali a sei voci*, respectively.

A gap in the record of salary payments at the Medici court occurs after 1571, but there is no reason to suppose that Striggio left their service during the 1570s. In the late 1560s he must have married Virginia Vagnoli of Siena, a singer and player of the *lirone* like himself.[14] Their third child, Alessandro, Jr., who was later to be the librettist for Monteverdi's *Orfeo*, was born in 1573. Striggio himself made another musical journey north to Austria and Bavaria in 1574, this time in the company of a young assistant called Giulio.[15] His presence in Mantua in 1574 is confirmed by letters he wrote to court officials there, in which he indicated he was returning (after his journey) to Medici service.[16] Being a nobleman and wealthy landowner in Mantua, Striggio had frequent contact there, often over matters of litigation with other members of his family. Throughout his twenty-eight-year period of service with the Medici, he spent a considerable amount of time in Mantua—as much as several months in any given year. Most of Striggio's known musical activities continue to point towards Florence, where his name appears once more at the head of a court list of musicians in 1579.[17] He took part in a further succession of celebrations, all of them weddings: that of Pellegrina Cappello and Ulisse Bentivoglio, in 1577;[18] of Bianca Cappello and Francesco de' Medici, in 1579;[19] (probably) of Eleonora de' Medici and Vincenzo Gonzaga, in 1584;[20] and of Virginia de' Medici and Cesare d'Este, in 1586.[21] Between 1584 and 1585 he played a crucial role in the transmission of musical practices then fashionable at Ferrara to the Florentine, and perhaps to the Mantuan, court. Having been invited by the Duke of Ferrara to spend two weeks at the Este court in the summer of 1584, Striggio was allowed to hear and examine the music of the renowed *concerto delle dame*; he described their virtuosic manner in letters to Florence, and sent examples of his own efforts to imitate it, receiving in turn fresh texts from the Medici court and annotations to his own compositions by Florence's virtuoso singer, Giulio Caccini.[22]

After April 1585, having completed in Mantua his musical commissions from both Grand Duke Francesco and Grand Duchess Bianca, Striggio resettled in Florence with his family.[23] When the festivities of the following year were over, he eventually decided to move back to his native city definitively, with his entire "family of fourteen or fifteen mouths," and so he left Florence on 12 April 1587.[24] Just a few months later Grand Duke Francesco was trying to entice him back. This time the composer refused the call, saying that the expenses of his family and his obligations to the duke of Mantua made a visit to Florence impossible.[25] He was present, however, at the wedding of the next grand duke, Ferdinando I, held in Florence in 1589: his name was recorded among those of the instrumentalists in the official edition of the *intermedi* music for the comedy, *La pellegrina*, as "il famoso Alessandro Striggio."[26]

From 1587, then, Striggio lived essentially in Mantua and served out the remaining five years of his life at the Gonzaga court, where he was listed in a court-roll as one of the *estraordinarii*.[27] On a memorial plaque of 1614, which his son Alessandro raised to his forebears, Striggio is named as *commensali* (a table companion) of Duke Guglielmo Gonzaga (d. 1587).[28] Striggio died on Saturday, 29 February 1592, after two weeks of fever, at the age of 55.[29] During the last twenty years of his life, Striggio's work appeared in print through many of the madrigal anthologies of the day. Four years after his death, between 1596 and 1597, his son Alessandro had printed three further collections of madrigals: *Il terzo libro, Il quarto libro,* and *Il quinto libro de madrigali a cinque voci.* The first two were dedicated to past patrons, but the *Quinto libro*, which appeared in 1597, has no dedication and no indication, as such, of its compiler.[30]

Praised by several contemporaries for his instrumental virtuosity and his compositional skill, Striggio was remembered beyond his own lifetime.[31] In 1612, a Mantuan writer, Eugenio Cagnani, gave him a prominent position in a short chronological account of Mantuan arts.[32] By 1635, however, G. B. Doni had praise only for *Il cicalamento delle donne al bucato.*[33] And when Dr. Burney came to consider Striggio in his historical survey, he found the madrigals he had transcribed (apparently from the *Primo libro . . . a sei voci*) "remarkable neither for genius or science."[34] In the nineteenth century, François-Joseph Fétis seems to have been the first to strike a positive note, however debatable, by saying that Striggio's principal talent lay in the expression of the meaning of words through the music and by linking him with Peri, Caccini, and Monteverdi.[35] Since then, Striggio's role in the pre-history of opera has been consistently emphasized.[36] Einstein's illuminating pages represent the only critical assessment of his madrigal production as a whole.[37]

Il primo libro de madrigali a sei voci

Striggio was almost exclusively a secular composer; his natural environment was that of the court. Historically, his name is linked with music for entertainment and festivity. He is the earliest of a number of composers, which includes Giovanni Croce, Orazio Vecchi, and Adriano Banchieri, to write in the genre of "madrigal comedy." Striggio's contributions to this genre, including the well-known *Cicalamento*, were published between 1567 and 1569. In its humorous intent and its mixture of musical styles, including the quotation of popular songs (both text and melody), the *Serenata* in the present collection was the immediate antecedent of these madrigal comedies. Of his music written for Medici festivals and other celebrations, only a small portion has survived: a few fragments in manuscript sources, some settings in his own madrigal collections (especially the posthumous ones), and several pieces in madrigal anthologies printed after 1571.[38] Striggio is the composer of seven individual madrigal collections in all, five of which survive complete. Apart from the posthumous books, whose contents were perhaps too heterogeneous or too outmoded by 1596 and 1597 to gain much favor, all of his publications enjoyed considerable success, in terms of reprint editions, during his lifetime—success comparable, in some respects, to that of Rore, Palestrina, and Lasso. Several individual settings, such as *Nasce la pena mia* (No. [2] in the present edition), gained particular fame, judging by the number of times it was reprinted in anthologies and by the variety of arrangements in manuscript and printed sources (see Critical Commentary).

First published in 1560, *Il primo libro de madrigali a sei voci* consisted of seventeen works (Nos. [1]–[17] of the present edition). Three additional madrigals (*madrigali aggiunti*) were added in successive printings of *Il primo libro . . . a sei voci*. Because the 1560 print is now lost, the music of this edition is transcribed, complete with the *madrigali aggiunti*, from a print issued in 1565 (see The Edition).

Striggio began his compositional career in the wake of the mid-century passion for Petrarch, represented most rigorously in the work of Willaert and Rore. However, Petrarchan texts, as such, are virtually absent from the varied contents of his *Primo libro de madrigali a cinque voci*, first printed at the same time as the *Primo libro . . . a sei voci*. For his contribution to the classic Petrarchan tradition, Striggio reserved the six-voice medium, the "most complex apparatus of the madrigal," as Einstein called it.[39] In some ways, however, Striggio's choice of Petrarchan texts in *Il primo libro . . . a sei voci* is less rigid than either Willaert's or Rore's. They had established the Petrarchan sonnet in a bipartite setting as the classic form of the madrigal. However, in the first thirteen works of *Il primo libro . . . a sei voci*, the range of Striggio's verse forms is broader and more at one with that of his immediate contemporaries. There are five complete sonnet settings (Nos. [1], [4], [11], [12], and [13]). Two of these are based on poems, both of which are Petrarchan in derivation, by Ariosto and Tansillo, respectively; the other three set poems by Petrarch himself. To these Striggio added settings of two sonnet octaves (Nos. [8] and [10]), a canzone stanza (No. [7]), and a sestina stanza (No. [9])—all by Petrarch—two *ottava rima* stanzas (No. [6]), and three shorter, in some ways less serious, madrigals (Nos. [2], [3], and [5]). Overall, however, Striggio's *Primo libro . . . a sei voci* maintains a literary weight comparable to that of Willaert's *Musica nova* and of Rore's early collections without repeating any of the same texts. Striggio may have been trying to avoid direct comparison, although in the case of the *risposta Anchor ch'io possa dire* (No. [3]), he was "answering" a famous Rore madrigal, *Anchor che col partire*. Indeed, at the opening of the first composition in the collection, *I dolci colli*, he cited the opening of one of Rore's most famous Petrarchan settings, the complete *Vergine* cycle, first published in 1548.[40]

Individual texts within almost any grouping of verses by Petrarch and by Petrarchists, are bound to share a number of poetic motifs. Obviously there is no question of imposing a unified poetic sequence on these first thirteen texts, which are arranged in *Il primo libro . . . a sei voci*, and in the present edition, as in most madrigal collections, according to the mode and clef arrangement of their settings. But there are a number of correspondences—in vocabulary, image, expression, and theme—that may suggest a certain conscious choice and arrangement of these thirteen pieces on the part of the composer; more so, certainly, than in the works of many of Striggio's contemporaries. In the early numbers a recurring emphasis falls on the con-

ventional theme of the lover's pain and suffering, caused above all by separation or absence from the beloved. This sentiment receives its quintessential statement in Bernardo Tasso's two *ottava rima* stanzas (set as No. [6]), one of the most celebrated rhetorical poems on the theme in the sixteenth century. Following this, the defeat of Reason before Love's compelling force becomes the focus of attention (Nos. [7]–[12]). Finally, Tansillo's *Poi che spiegat'ho l'ale* (No. [13]), whose text is an affirmation of poetical genius and of the value of the poet's work, a theme already hinted at in Nos. [9] and [10], makes a positive conclusion to this group of madrigals.

What follows is quite different in textual and musical terms: three lighter settings (Nos. [14]–[16]), characterized by the discursive rhythms of the *canzone alla francese* and triple-time interjections. These pieces prepare the way, as it were, for the book's final (in its original, 1560, form) number, which was labeled as a *serenata*. After the madrigalesque depiction of a nocturnal scene, text and music are interrupted by a popular song, and then gradually the text degenerates into the long-winded complaints of a Petrarchan serenader. Interwoven are popular songs and citations of contemporary madrigals; the situations presented recall those of the *canzone villanesca alla napolitana*.[41] In many ways, the *Serenata*, whose text is pure *poesia per musica*, combining the most heterogeneous materials, turns the lofty sentiments of the serious Petrarch settings inside out; in the context of the whole collection, this final work acts as a foil to the rest. The comedy lies almost entirely in the exaggeration and parody of serious emotions.[42]

In some contrast to the derivation of his literary choices, Striggio's musical style in the serious settings in *Il primo libro . . . a sei voci* does not closely follow that of Willaert's *Musica nova* or that of Rore's first two collections (1542, 1544). There, a style of both strict and, above all, free imitation prevails.[43] However, by the 1550s, even Rore himself was moving towards a more chordal style, and a homophonic idiom was a feature of many madrigalists' work. Striggio, a virtuoso on a pre-eminently chordal instrument, was no exception to this tendency. In the *Primo libro . . . a sei voci*, he ranged from strict and free imitation to pure and rhythmically animated homophony within any one setting. Several of his textures form a complex mixture of imitation and homophony, a complexity made possible by having six voices at hand: see, for example, the openings of Nos. [1] and [11]. Einstein thought Striggio's counterpoint was "basically homophonic in its motivation";[44] but although Striggio often adopted an animated chordal style, he was equally capable of creating a genuine imitative movement in six real parts.

As might be expected for a madrigalist of his time, Striggio employed the more traditional measure, the *misura di breve* (₵), almost exclusively, as if to emphasize the traditional aspects of his style.[45] But with the exception of *Lasciat'hai, Morte* (No. [4], set to the gloomiest text in the collection), his use of this measure is often more apparent than real. In general he seems to have taken his cue in the use of measure from such examples as Rore's *Terzo libro de madrigali a cinque voci* (1548) and his *Primo libro de madrigali a quattro voci* (1550). Einstein picked out *Anchor che col partire* from Rore's latter collection, noting there a new freedom of tempo, a flexibility in the use of fast and slow motion.[46] It is significant, therefore, that Striggio's *Primo libro . . . a sei voci* includes a *risposta* (No. [3]) to Rore's composition that is also characterized by the freedom of tempo and flexibility in fast and slow motion mentioned above. With regard to Striggio, Einstein spoke of a "hovering" between the *misura di breve* (¢) and the *misura comune* (C) as characteristic of his style.[47] But this does not betoken indecision on Striggio's part; rather, it indicates the presence of strong rhythmic contrasts, even the superimposition of different rhythmic figures, in his work. Such features appear in the madrigals of his contemporaries, of course; but the effect, for example, of the "acceleration" in some of the animated contrapuntal conclusions in Striggio's music is especially striking.

Another area in which Striggio may be considered traditional, perhaps more controversially, is that of mode and harmony. To one writer, Ray J. Tadlock, he appeared quite conservative in his use of dissonance and chromaticism, the implication being a certain lack of expressiveness in his music.[48] But, as Nino Pirrotta has pointed out, dissonance and chromaticism have by no means the monopoly on expression.[49] Striggio's style can, at most, be said to be relatively conservative, and it is generally at one with the conventional musical language of his time. In considering his modal and harmonic vocabulary, it is necessary to see what seem to be mild dissonances and innocuous progressions in their proper context: a basically consonant idiom built, from a harmonic standpoint, on chords in their root position with bass movement most common between intervals of a fourth and fifth. On the other hand, the interest expressed by some of Striggio's contemporaries in chromaticism and their pronounced use of dissonance and false relations do not find a strong echo in the *Primo libro . . . a sei voci*. Einstein's description of the "delicate rarefied harmony"[50] of *Nasce la pena miu* (No. [2]) probably refers to an overall control of relatively simple means. The infrequent but refined use of B-flats, the few suspended ninths, and the shift to C at "Ahi vita triste e frale" (m. 46) after a cadence in D stand out from the whole as expressive means. In general, a more developed harmonic language is encountered in *Amor, io fallo* (No. [11]), with its prominent false

relations at the opening, skillful use of E-flats, and more consistent use of dissonance. By contrast, the modesty of the alternating chords of E and A for the first fourteen measures of *Lasciat'hai, Morte* (No. [4]) makes the characterization of "Oscuro et freddo" with a new G tone (m. 15) all the more chilling.

It would be wrong, however, to consider Striggio's style in terms of its harmonic expression alone. For Pirrotta, "Striggio's artistry lies largely in the wealth of contrapuntal invention which he manages to develop even within the bounds of quite precisely defined harmonies."[51] This richness is maximized in the six-voice medium, for example, in many of the concluding sections of the settings. The setting of a final line or couplet frequently occupies a relatively disproportionate section of a whole composition. In general, the virtuosity of the combination of melodies is more remarkable than the melodies themselves. As may be said of Willaert, and to a lesser extent of Rore, Striggio is not a great melodist. When his music is compared to that of Rore and Willaert, it shows that Striggio did not always attain their masterly rhythmic agility, despite his expertise at introducing triple-time cross-rhythms, and he appears to have been somewhat more conditioned than they by the madrigalist's conventional response to words according to the precepts of *imitazione della natura*. By 1560 there was a veritable arsenal of such illustrative devices available to madrigalists. Although in the *Primo libro . . . a sei voci* Striggio did sometimes use word-painting in a thoroughgoing manner—it is a trait he was to develop later, especially in his *Secondo libro de madrigali a sei voci* (1571)—overall, it seems that he was less concerned with depicting, as such, than he was with suggesting an atmosphere or mood. The rhetorical grandiloquence of Bernardo Tasso's text in *Se ben di sette stell'ardent'e belle* (No. [6]) is reflected in the boldness of the setting's melodies, in its breadth of phrase and contrapuntal treatment, and in the richness of the six-voice texture at key phrases, such as "L'interna pena" ("The internal torment"; mm. 148–56).

The formal control which Striggio brought to bear on his material is a further indication of his concern with seeing his composition as a whole and not merely as a series of madrigalisms. Apart from his ability to extend his musical ideas to considerable length, he was capable of, and partial to, composition involving the continual variation of single melodic figures. Several settings would merit examination from this point of view; if we remember the Rorean derivation of *Anchor ch'io possa dire* (No. [3]), this emphasis on melodic variation is hardly surprising. For example, Striggio exploited a most conventional melodic tag to a remarkable extent in *Madonna, poich'occidermi volete* (No. [5]), giving that playful text a musical weight that almost justifies its presence among texts by Petrarch and the Petrarchists. On a larger scale, textual symmetries and repetitions in the *Serenata* (No. [17])—indications, perhaps, of its character as *poesia per musica*—create the possibility of a balanced and coherent musical setting.

The integrity of the original edition (issued in 1560 and now lost) of the *Primo libro de madrigali a sei voci* was partly obscured by the addition of three *madrigali aggiunti* to successive prints. The first of these *aggiunti*, by Striggio himself, is an occasional composition. The other two come from madrigalists, active in Venice, who represent two different generations: Perissone Cambio (ca. 1520–late 1560s) is associated with the group attached to Willaert in the 1540s; Claudio Merulo (1533–1604—listed as "Claudio da Correggio" in the 1565 source partbooks) belonged to the following generation. Merulo's piece, *L'alma mia fiamma* (No. [19]), apparently his first published madrigal, shows him to be, like Striggio, a follower of Petrarchan fashions; but he was even more tied to the traditional measure. The text set by Cambio, *Anchor che col partire* (No. [20]), was made famous in a setting by Rore (discussed above); but Cambio's composition bears comparison well. Beyond the fact that these *aggiunti* are a part of the transcription source, their historical interest and musical qualities make them worthy of inclusion in the present edition.

Performance Practice

Striggio's *Primo libro . . . a sei voci* has the standard arrangement of settings according to "low key" clefs (*chiavi naturali*: C_1, C_3, C_4, F_4 or F_3) and "high key" clefs (*chiavette*: G_2, C_2, C_3, F_3 or C_4) for canto, alto, tenore, and basso. While *chiavi naturali* pieces (Nos. [1]–[5], [7], [9]–[12], and [20]) may be performed comfortably at written pitch, the *chiavette* madrigals (Nos. [6], [8], and [13]–[19]) would, following sixteenth-century conventions, be transposed downwards by as much as a perfect fourth.[52] As there were no absolute standards of pitch during this period, the interval of transposition need not be fixed rigidly; but, in view of the high *tessiture* especially of canto and tenore parts in these settings, downward transposition is certainly recommendable.

Given their printed format in partbooks with full textual underlay, we might assume that these madrigals were conceived for and performed by a purely vocal ensemble. Performance by such ensembles is entirely feasible, but there is much evidence in a variety of sixteenth-century sources, including paintings and engraved illustrations, that instrumental participation was frequent in the performance of vocal music. The use of instruments may seem especially appropriate in

the case of madrigals by Striggio since, as an instrumental virtuoso, he is known to have taken part in performances of his own music, presumably playing the small or large *lira* or the lute.[53] The number of arrangements of madrigals in the *Primo libro . . . a sei voci*, listed in the Critical Commentary, underlines this possibility. Both the original partbooks and the present edition's score format should perhaps best be regarded as a starting-point for performances realized with instrumental participation. The number of possibilities is considerable. A few may be mentioned here: a six-part vocal ensemble doubled by viols;[54] solo voice with lute or *lira* accompaniment; a mixed ensemble of voices and instruments, perhaps after the model of Striggio's "orchestration" for *intermedi* performances during the 1560s.[55]

The Edition

The first edition of the *Primo libro de madrigali a sei voci* (1560) has not survived, and examples of the first two known prints exist incomplete: that of 1560 exists in the canto, alto, and sesto parts only; that of 1561 exists in the quinto part only. The present edition is based on the third known print, issued by Gardano in 1565, which does survive complete. Two copies exist, one in the Civico Museo Bibliografico Musicale, Bologna (used here), the other in the Library of Congress in Washington, D.C. The 1565 print was checked against the surviving parts of the 1560 edition and against the single surviving part of the 1561 edition: any musical differences among the three prints have been noted in the Critical Commentary.

In general, the 1565 print is accurate and close in most respects to the earlier prints. Although many later editions were consulted, the 1565 print was not collated with all subsequent prints because these reveal an increasing number of errors in the music, a less-full text—both regarding elisions and the use of the *ij* repetition symbol—and an increased use of *musica ficta*. A list of all prints is given in the Sources section; but except for a few particular readings, the variants listed in the Critical Commentary itself refer only to the 1560, 1561, and 1565 prints.

In the present edition, an incipit shows the original clef, key- and time-signature, and first note of the piece for each voice part. The edition retains original note values, except in sections of triple-time, where these values have been reduced by half: the proportional relation between duple and triple time is indicated editorially above the staff. Source ligatures and coloration are represented by the conventional modern signs (⌐‾‾ and ⌐ ¬). The final note of each piece, notated as a *longa* in the print, appears in the edition as a note equivalent in duration to a whole measure, with a fermata placed above. Barlines have been introduced throughout in what has seemed to be the best representation of Striggio's "hovering" between the *misura di breve* and the *misura comune*: that is, in measures of two half-note beats with the signature ¢. The single exception to this, the *seconda parte* of No. [12], retains the original C indication in the modern edition: in context, this implies a reduced tempo of four quarter-note beats to the measure. All accidentals that appear in the source print have been reproduced in the edition, even where they seem superfluous by modern convention. The modern natural sign has been introduced in place of the sharp sign used in the print to indicate the cancellation of a flat sign. Source accidentals are assumed to apply to all immediate repetitions of the same pitch. When a modern barline intervenes in such a repetition, the accidental has been repeated on the staff and enclosed in brackets. All editorial accidentals appear above the staff and apply only to the single note directly below them. If they serve a cautionary function, they are enclosed in parentheses. Square brackets also enclose other editorial material.

The poetic text used in the present edition follows the source closely as regards spelling: any variation is noted in the Critical Commentary. However, capitalization has been made regular, and all punctuation and accents—both practically absent from the source—are editorial. They have been tacitly added in consultation with sixteenth-century and modern editions of the poems. In the case of the *Serenata* (No. [17]), which presents particular problems, further citations of editorial intervention are given in the Critical Commentary. Textual variations among voice-parts have been tacitly regularized according to the version most frequently found in the source. Where the repetition symbol *ij* is found in the source, the modern edition presents the full text enclosed with square brackets.

Sources

The 1565 Gardano reprint of *Il primo libro de madrigali a sei voci* is the primary source for the present edition. Other, concordant, sources are listed below, together with the *sigla* by which they are cited in the Critical Commentary.

Manuscript Sources

The nature of these sources—their relatively late date in many cases, their incompleteness in others, and the fact that several are arrangements—has precluded their use in the preparation of the musical text in this edition. They are listed below, together with a citation of the madrigals here with which they are concordant, to give an idea of the diffusion of the madrigals in the book.

BolC Q34	Bologna, Civico Museo Bibliografico Musicale, MS Q34, *Spartitura generale . . . Joannes Amigonus . . . 1613*; score, without textual underlay. Nos. [2] and [9]
BolC C33	Bologna, Civico Museo Bibliografico Musicale, MS C.33, *Il dolcimelo d'Aurelio Virgiliano, dove si contengono variati passaggi, e diminutioni cosi per voci, come per tutte sorte d'instrumenti musicali; con loro accordi, e modi di sonare*; diminution manual, mensural notation, ca. 1600. See Gaetano Gaspari, *Catalogo della Biblioteca del Liceo musicale di Bologna*, 4 vols. (Bologna, 1890–1905; reprint, Bologna; Formi, 1961), 1:341; and Imogene Horsley, "The Solo Ricercar in Diminution Manuals: New Light on Early Wind and String Techniques," *Acta musicologica* 33 (1961): 33. No. [2]
BruCR 27089	Brussels, Bibliothèque du Conservatoire Royale, MS 27.089, choirbook, ca. 1600. See Charles Van den Borren, "Inventaire des manuscrits de musique polyphonique qui se trouvent en Belgique," *Acta musicologica* 5 (1933): 177–83. No. [2]
CraJ 40032	Cracow, Biblioteka Jagiellońska, MS formerly in Königliche Hausbibliothek, Berlin (now Staatsbibliothek Preussicher Kulturbesitz) with call-number Mus. ms. 40.032 (*olim* Z 32); sixteenth-century lute book. No. [2]
FlorBN LF2	Florence, Biblioteca Nazionale Centrale, Fondo Landau-Finaly MS Mus. 2; supplement to Vincenzo Galilei's *Fronimo* (Venice, 1568). See Claude V. Palisca, "Vincenzo Galilei's Arrangements for Voice and Lute," in *Essays in Musicology in Honor of Dragon Plamenac* (Pittsburgh: University of Pittsburgh Press, 1969), pp. 228–31; lute tablature. Nos. [3] and [6]
FlorML 641	Florence, Biblioteca Medicea Laurenziana, Acquisti e doni 641, *Intavolatura di M. Alamanno Aiolli* (1565–90); keyboard tablature. See Frank A. D'Accone, "The *Intavolatura di M. Alamanno Aiolli*," *Musica disciplina* 20 (1966): 151–74. No. [2]
LegT	According to the catalogue of Ernst Pfudel, *Die Musik-Handschriften der*

Königl. Ritter-Akademie zu Liegnitz (Leipzig, 1886), three manuscripts in the former Bibliothek Rudolfina in Liegnitz contained madrigals, or arrangements of madrigals, by Striggio. These were: MS 20 (Lib. No. 52), 6 partbooks; MS 24 (Lib. No. 58), 8 partbooks; MS 31 (Lib. No. 99)—MS 31 is a German organ tablature. Pfudel gives no information about dates or provenance. These manuscripts may now be located in Legnica (Liegnitz), Biblioteka Towarzystwa Przjaciól Nauk. At present, the editor is unable to confirm or deny this, despite attempts to communicate with the library. In the Critical Commentary, these manuscripts are referred to, with an indication of doubt, as LegT 20, LegT 24, and LegT 31, respectively. Nos. [2], [4], [6], [9], [10], [11], [12], and [14]

LonBL 30491   London, British Library, Additional MS 30491; miscellaneous collection of vocal music, four-part instrumental pieces, and diminutions for the *viola bastarda*; early seventeenth century. See Augustus Hughes-Hughes, *Catalogue of Manuscript Music in the British Museum*, 3 vols. (London, 1906–9; reprint, London: British Museum, 1964–66), 2:225; 3:157, 204. No. [2]

MilBC Tarasconi   Milan, Biblioteca del Conservatorio Giuseppe Verdi, the "Tarasconi Codex"; score, with texts under or beside music (not underlaid), probably compiled 1586–88. See Guglielmo Barblan and Agostina Zecca Laterza, "The Tarasconi Codex in the Library of the Milan Conservatory," *The Musical Quarterly* 60 (1974): 195–221. Nos. [2], [3], [4], [6], [9], [11], and [14]

ModE C311   Modena, Biblioteca Estense, MS Mus. C.311, *Libro di Cosimo Bottegari . . . arie e canzoni in musica* (1573–74); lute intablature. See Carol MacClintock, "A Court Musician's Song Book: Modena MS. 311," *Journal of the American Musicological Society* 9 (1956): 177–92; Cosimo Bottegari, *The Bottegari Lutebook*, ed. Carol MacClintock (Wellesley, Mass.: Broude Bros., 1965). No. [12]

MunBS 218   Munich, Bayerische Staatsbibliothek, MS 218 (*olim* Mus. MS 259), version of Michael Herrer's *Hortus musicalis . . . liber II* (Munich: A. Berg, 1609), dated 1628; score. [No. 2]

ParBN 851   Paris, Bibliothèque Nationale, Res. Vma. Ms. 851, known as "The Bourdeney Manuscript," score with underlay; compiled late sixteenth century. See Oscar Mischiati, "Un'antologia manoscritta in partitura del secolo XVI. Il Ms. Bourdeney della Bibliothèque Nationale di Parigi," *Rivista italiana di musicologia* 10 (1975): 265–328. Nos. [2] and [3]

PelpS 305   Pelplin, Biblioteka Seminarium, MS 305, one of six separately bound MSS (Nos. 304–8, 308a), known as "The Pelplin Tablature," dated 1620–30; organ tablature. See Adam Sutkowski and Alina Osostowicz-Sutkowska, eds., *The Pelplin Tabulature. A Thematic Catalogue*, Antiquitates musicae in Polonia, vol. 1 (Warsaw-Graz: Warsaw University Press, 1963), pp. 108–9; see vol. 3, *Facsimile. Part 2* (1965), pp. 98–99. No. [2]

RegB 775   Regensburg, Bischöfliche Zentralbibliothek, MS Antiquitates Ratisbonenses 775, *Autores diversi . . . 1579*; 6 partbooks. Nos. [1], [2], [3], [4], [5], [6], [7], [8], and [20]

TübU 40034   Tübingen, Universitätsbibliothek, Mus. MS 40034, Christoph Löffelholtz von Kolberg, *Tablaturbuch*; keyboard tablature (new German tablature); formerly in Deutsche Staatsbibliothek, Berlin, with call-number Mus. MS 40.034 (*olim* Z 34). See Wilhelm Merian, *Der Tanz in den deutschen Tablaturbüchern* (Leipzig, 1927; reprint, Hildesheim: Olms, 1968), pp. 171, 289f. No. [2]

UppU 409   Uppsala, Universitetsbiblioteket, Instr. mus. hs. 409 (*olim* 408), Gustavus Duben, *Keyboard Tablature Book* (1641); German organ tablature. See Åke Davidsson. "The Origin of the Collections of Old Music in Swedish Libraries," *Nordisk Tidskrift för Bok- och Biblioteksväsen*, 49 (1962): 112ff. No. [2]

UtrR Lerma   Utrecht, Bibliotheek der Rijksuniversiteit, *Codex Lerma*; choirbook from ducal chapel of Lerma, near Burgos, in Spain, dated between 1600 and 1620. See Willem Elders, "The Lerma Codex: a Newly Discovered Choirbook from Seventeenth-Century Spain," *Tijdschrift van de Vereniging voor Nederlandse Muziekgeschiedenis*, 20/4 (1967): 187–205; 198. Nos. [2], [3], [8], [9], [11], [12], [13], [14], and [16]

WarU Olkuz   Warsaw, Biblioteka Uniwersytecka, two partbooks (quinto and basso), once belonging to the church of St. Andrew in Olkuz, dated ca. 1579. See Mirosław Perz, "Rekopiśmienne Partesy Olkuskie," *Muzyka*, 14/2 (1969): 18–45; 36. No. [2]

WroU 51335   Wrocław, Biblioteka Uniwersytecka, MS 51335 Muz., miscellaneous collection of MSS and music prints (dated 1575–81) bound together: discanto, altus, primo tenor (= tenore?), basso, quinto parts only. Formerly in deposit as WroU 51435 below, with call-number Br. Mus. K. 54; in Friedrich Kuhn, *Beschreibendes Verzeichnis der alten Musikalien–Handschriften und Druckwerke–des Kgl. Gymnasiums zu Brieg* (Leipzig: Breitkopf & Härtel, 1897), p. 19. No. [2]

WroU 51435   Wrocław, Biblioteka Uniwersytecka, MS 51435 Muz., miscellaneous collection of MSS and music prints (dated 1571–75) bound together: discanto, alto, tenor (= sesto?), tenor parts only. Formerly in deposit in the Königliche und Universitäts-Bibliothek, Breslau: Leihgabe des Kgl. Gymnasiums in Brieg, with call-number Br. Mus. K. 28. See Friedrich Kuhn, *Beschreibendes Verzeichnis der alten Musikalien–Handschriften und Druckwerke–des Kgl. Gymnasiums zu Brieg* (Leipzig, Breitkopf & Härtel, 1897), p. 38. MS at Wrocław (Breslau) since 1945. No. [2]

Printed Sources

Given below is information taken from the title pages of all known reprints and re-editions (the original edition not having survived) of the *Primo libro . . . a sei voci*: this includes the place of publication, printer, and the date of publication. This information is supplemented, after each listing, by details of format and RISM references where applicable. For the prints issued after 1560, an indication (e.g., "contents = 1560") documents the order in which the madrigals (excluding the *aggiunti*) appear in each edition by comparing that order against a previously described order.

1. [1560] DI ALESSANDRO STRIGGIO / GENTIL'HVOMO MANTOVANO SERVITORE / dell'Illustriss. & Eccellentiss. Cosmo de Medici Duca di Firenze, è di Siena. Il Primo libro de / Madregali a sei uoci Nouamente per Antonio Gardano con Noua gionta Ristampato. / *A SEI* [printer's device] *VOCI / In Venetia Appresso di / Antonio Gardano. / 1560.*
Octavo, obl.; RISM 1560^{22}.

2. [1561] DI ALESSANDRO STRIGGIO / GENTIL'HVOMO MANTOVANO / Servitore dell'Illustriss. & Eccellentiss. Cosmo de Medici / Duca di Firenze, è di Siena. / *Il primo libro de Madregali a sei voci Nouamente con gionta Ristampato.* / [printer's device] / *In Venegia Appresso Girolamo Scotto. 1561.*
Octavo, obl.; contents = 1560.

3. [1565] DI ALESSANDRO STRIGGIO / GENTIL'HVOMO MANTOVANO SERVITORE / dell'Illustriss. & Eccellentiss. Cosmo de Medici Duca di Firenze, è di Siena. Il primo libro de / Madrigali a sei uoci Nouamente per antonio Gardano con noua gionta Ristampato. / A SEI [printer's device] VOCI / In Venetia Appresso di / Antonio Gardano. / 1565.
Octavo, obl.; contents = 1560; RISM 1565^{19}. This is the source used for the present edition: see Plate I.

4. [1566] DI ALESSANDRO STRIGGIO / GENTIL'HVOMO MANTOVANO / IL PRIMO libro delli Madrigali a SEI uoci, / Nouamente con noua gionta ristampato / [printer's device] / IN VINEGIA M. D. LXVI. / APPRESSO GIROLAMO SCOTTO.
Octavo; contents: order rearranged, lacks No. [20]; RISM 1566^{19}.

5. [1566] DI ALESSANDRO STRIGGIO / GENTIL'HVOMO MANTOVANO SERVITORE / DELL'ILLUSTRISS. ET ECCELLENTISS. COSMO DE MEDICI / DUCA DI FIRENZE, E DI SIENA. / Il primo Libro de Madrigali a sei uoci, Nouamente con una noua giunta Ristampato. / A SEI [printer's device] VOCI / IN VENETIA. [On the end-leaf:] In Venetia appresso Francesco Rampazetto. / MDLXVI.
Octavo, obl.; contents = 1560; RISM 1566^{20}.

6. [1569] DI ALESSANDRO STRIGGIO / GENTIL'HVOMO MANTOVANO SERVITORE / dell'Illustriss. & Eccellentiss. Cosmo de Medici Duca di Firenze, è/ di Siena. Il Primo libro de/

Madregali a sei uoci Nouamente per Antonio Gardano con Noua gionta Ristampato. / A SEI [printer's device] VOCI / In Venetia Appresso di / Antonio Gardano. / 1569.
Octavo, obl.; contents = 1560; RISM 1569[34].

7. [1578] IL PRIMO LIBRO / DELLI MADRIGALI A SEI VOCI / DI M. ALESSANDRO STRIGGIO / Gentil'huomo Mantouano. / *Nouamente ristampato.* / [printer's device] / *IN VINEGGIA.* / Appresso l'herede di Girolamo Scotto. / *MDLXXVIII.*
Octavo; contents = 1560; RISM 1578[23].

8. [1579] DI ALESSANDRO STRIGGIO / GENTIL'HVOMO MANTOVANO / IL PRIMO LIBRO DE MADRIGALI / A SEI VOCI, / Nouamente per Angelo Gardano con ogni diligenza Ristampati. / [printer's device] / In Venetia Appresso / Angelo Gardano. / 1579.
Octavo; contents: order rearranged, lacks Nos. [18]–[20], i.e., the *aggiunti.*

9. [1585] DI ALESSANDRO STRIGGIO / *GENTIL'HVOMO MANTOVANO* / IL PRIMO LIBRO DE MADRIGALI / A SEI VOCI / *Nouamente ristampato.* / [printer's device] / IN VINEGIA Appresso l'Herede di Girolamo Scotto. / *MDLXXXV.*
Octavo; contents = 1579.

10. [1592] DI ALESSANDRO STRIGGIO / GENTIL'HVOMO MANTOVANO / IL PRIMO LIBRO / De Madrigali a Sei Voci. / [ornament] / Nouamente con ogni diligenza Ristampato. / [printer's device] / In Venetia Appresso Angelo Gardano. / M. D. / LXXXXII.
Octavo; contents = 1579.

Acknowledgments

In the preparation of this edition, several people and institutions have helped and encouraged me. I am grateful, first, to Dr. Sergio Paganelli, the former librarian of the Civico Museo Bibliografico Musicale, Bologna, for permission to use the library's copy of the *Primo libro de madrigali a sei voci* for this edition, and also for permission to reproduce two pages from the original print. Similarly, I wish to thank the Musiksammlung of the Österreichische Nationalbibliothek, Vienna, for supplying me with a microfilm of two parts of the 1560 edition; Dr. Enrico Paganuzzi, librarian of the Accademia Filarmonica of Verona, for allowing me to check the alto part of the 1560 edition in the library of the Accademia; and the Bibliothèque of the Musée Condé, Chantilly, for supplying me with a microfilm of the quinto part of the 1561 edition. In addition, the staffs of libraries in Berlin, Brussels, Cracow, London, Regensburg, Uppsala, and Wrocław generously responded to my questions concerning manuscript sources of Striggio madrigals.

My research into the biography of Striggio has been greatly aided by the kindness of the *direttrice* of the Archivio di Stato in Mantua, Dottoressa Adele Bellù; and I am grateful to Don Giancarlo Manzoli of the Archivio Diocesano, Mantua, for his help in the search for Striggio's birthdate. Dr. Iain Fenlon of Cambridge and Professor Denis Arnold of Oxford were both helpful with advice and information about the Mantuan archives. In making translations of the texts, I owe much to Isabella Pellicanò and to Christopher Whyte; the final result is, of course, my own responsibility. In matters more adherent to the music, I have benefited from discussions with James Chater; and my gratitude in this respect goes above all to Dr. Frederick Sternfeld of Oxford, for his initial encouragement and continuing support.

David S. Butchart

Notes

1. The most recent studies to include discussion of Striggio's work are: Wolfgang Osthoff, *Theatergesang und darstellende Musik in der italienischen Renaissance* (Tutzing: Schneider, 1969), 1:332–56; Howard Mayer Brown, *Sixteenth-Century Instrumentation: the Music for the Florentine Intermedi*, American Institute of Musicology, Musicological Studies and Documents, vol. 30 (Neuhausen-Stuttgart: Hänssler, 1973), pp. 96–107; and Nino Pirrotta, *Li due Orfei*, rev. ed. (Turin: Einaudi, 1975), published in English as *Music and Theatre from Poliziano to Monteverdi* (Cambridge: Cambridge University Press, 1982). Reference here is made to the 1975 edition. Recent articles by the present editor are referred to below.

2. Luigi Torchi included five Striggio madrigals from later anthology collections in *L'arte musicale in Italia* (Milan: Ricordi, 1897), 1:333–62. In Philippe de Monte, *Missa Nasce la pena mia* in *Opera*, vol. 10, ed. Charles Van den Borren and Julius Van Nuffel (Düsseldorf: Schwann, 1929; reprint, New York: Broude Brothers, 1965), a supplement includes *Nasce la pena mia*, the madrigal by Striggio on which the mass is based. Two madrigals in the present edition, *Nasce la pena mia* (No. [2]) and *Anchor ch'io possa dire* (No. [3]), along with vocal diminution arrangements based on them, are included in Richard Erig and Veronika Gutmann, *Italienische Diminutionen. Die zwischen 1553 and 1638 mehrmals bearbeiteten Sätze* (Zürich: Päuler, 1979), pp. 291–305 and 211–23,

respectively. Single madrigals are included in Denis Arnold, ed., *Vier Madrigale von mantuaner Komponisten zu 5 und 8 Stimmen*, Das Chorwerk, vol. 80 (Wolfenbüttel: Möseler, 1961), pp. 27–34 (*Mentre l'un polo intorno, a8*); Osthoff, *Theatergesang*, 2:122–31 (*A me che fatta, son negletta e sola*); Howard Mayer Brown, "Psyche's Lament: Some Music for the Medici Wedding of 1565" in *Words and Music . . . in Honor of A. Tillman Merritt* (Cambridge, Mass.: Harvard University Press, 1972), pp. 17–28 (*Fuggi, speme mia, fuggi*); Iain Fenlon, *Music and Patronage in Sixteenth-Century Mantua* (Cambridge: Cambridge University Press, 1980–82), 2:72–77 (*Hor che le stelle in cielo*). There are Italian editions of two of the "madrigal comedies": Bonaventura Somma, ed., *Il cicalamento delle donne al bucato* (Rome: De Santis, 1947); and Federico Mompellio, ed., *La caccia* (Rome: De Santis, 1972). See also Alfred Einstein, *The Italian Madrigal* (Princeton: Princeton University Press, 1949; reprint, Princeton: Princeton University Press, 1971), 3:285–94, for the other "madrigal comedy," *Il gioco di primiera*.

3. Striggio's approximate birthdate can be derived from the information contained in the registration of his death: see n. 29 below.

4. Archivio di Stato, Mantua (hereafter ASMN), Archivio notarile, *Estensioni* 1547, fol. 1370r.

5. Einstein, *The Italian Madrigal*, 2:761, 765. A possible candidate as Striggio's teacher is Roberto Avanzini (or Roberto da Rimini), active in Mantua as singer, lutenist, and player of the *violone* from 1512 to his death in 1560. See Pietro Canal, *Della musica a Mantova* (Venice, 1881) extract of *Memorie del Reale Istituto Veneto di scienze, lettere e arti*, vol. 21 (reprint, Bologna: Forni, 1977), pp. 22–23; Antonino Bertolotti, *Musici alla corte dei Gonzaga in Mantova dal secolo XV al XVIII* (Milan, 1890; reprint, Bologna: Forni, 1969), pp. 21–22; and Fenlon, *Music and Patronage*, 1:67–68.

6. Archivio di Stato, Florence (hereafter ASF), Mediceo del principato 631, fol. 3v. Subsequent payments are recorded in ibid., Depositeria generale 1515, *Salariati 1560*, fol. 59.

7. One is in Francesco Sansovino's *Delle cento novelle scelte da' più nobili scrittori della lingua volgare* (Venice: Sansovino, 1561; reprint, 1563), p. 394r. Sansovino sets his scene in Venice in 1556, during a time of plague. After the ninth day's tales, the company enjoys music, and a certain Virginia is praised both for her singing and for her playing of the *violone*, in which "ella non cede né ad Alfonso né allo Strigghia ch'è così famoso in questa materia" ("she does not concede anything at all either to Alfonso [Dalla Viola] or to Striggio, who is so renowned in this art"). The other reference is in Cosimo Bartoli's *Ragionamenti accademici . . . sopra alcuni luoghi difficili di Dante* (Venice: Franceschi, 1567), p. 37ᵇ: "Io havevo in vero sentito molto lodare uno Alessandro strigia da Mantova, non solo eccellente, ma eccellentissimo nel sonar la viola: e far sentir in essa quatro parti a un tratto con tanta leggiadria e con tanta musica, che fa stupire gli ascoltanti, et oltre a questo le sue compositioni son così musicali e buone, come altre che in questi tempi si sentino." ("In truth, I have heard much praised one Alessandro Striggio from Mantua; he is not only good but exceptional at playing the 'viola' and can play four parts on it at once with such elegance and skill that he astonishes the listeners. And besides that, his compositions are considered as musical and as good as any others that we hear these days.") Although this book was published in 1567, its material goes back more than twenty years in places. The passage concerning Striggio refers to a time before his arrival in Florence; and from the rest of the discussion a date around 1554 or 1555 may be postulated.

8. On the *lira da braccio*, see Emanuel Winternitz, "The Lira da braccio," in *Musical Instruments and Their Symbolism in Western Art* (New Haven and London: Yale University Press, 1967; reprint, New Haven: Yale University Press, 1979), pp. 86–98. Striggio's *lirone* was an especially splendid example, according to the account written by the musical theorist Gerolamo Cardano: "We have seen Striggio's *lira*. It is as tall and thick as a man and somewhat wider. The rose is close to the fingerboard so that it can scarcely be seen. The *lira* was constructed with eighteen strings. Its body is rounded with uncurved sides and the fingerboard is a little longer than the body. . . .[The tuning] exceeds the range of any man-made instrument and extends higher than any human tone." See Clement A. Miller, ed., *Hieronymus Cardanus (1501–1576): Writings on Music*, American Institute of Musicology, Musicological Studies and Documents, vol. 32 (Neuhausen-Stuttgart: Hänssler, 1973), pp. 178ff.

9. Letter of Striggio to Duke Cosimo de' Medici, Florence, 25 February 1560, in ASF, Mediceo del principato 483a, fol. 645r. Reprinted in David S. Butchart, "The First Published Compositions of Alessandro Striggio," *Studi musicali* 12 (1983): 26.

10. Letter of Striggio to Duke Guglielmo Gonzaga, Venice, 1 June 1560, in ASMN, Archivio Gonzaga (hereafter AG) 1493. Reprinted in Butchart, "The First Published Compositions," p. 27.

11. For further bibliographical information, see Federico Ghisi, *Feste musicali della Firenze medicea (1480–1589)* (Florence: Vallecchi, 1939), pp. xxv–xxxiv; and Brown, *Sixteenth-Century Instrumentation*, pp. 96–105.

12. On the 1567 journey, see David S. Butchart, "A Musical Journey of 1567: Alessandro Striggio in Vienna, Munich, Paris and London," *Music & Letters* 63 (1982): 1–16.

13. For a description of the 1568 Munich festivities, see Massimo Troiano, *Dialoghi . . .* (Venice: Zaltieri, 1569), pp. 52 and 146.

14. She is, by coincidence, the Virginia mentioned by Sansovino in his *Cento novelle*: see n. 7 above. On Virginia, see Alfredo Saviotti, "Un'artista del Cinquecento: Virginia Vagnoli da Siena," *Bullettino Senese di storia patria* 26 (1919): 105–34.

15. See, among others, letter of Emperor Maximilian II to Guglielmo Gonzaga, Vienna, 1 September 1574, in ASMN, AG 431; and letter of Duke Albrecht of Bavaria to Francesco de' Medici, Freiburg, 10 October 1574, in ASF, Mediceo del principato 4281, unfoliated. See also Adolf Sandberger, *Beiträge zur Geschichte der bayerischen Hofkapelle unter Orlando di Lasso* (Leipzig: Breitkopf & Härtel, 1894–95; reprint, Wiesbaden: Sändig, 1973), p. 73, for a record of a payment made to Striggio by the Bavarian court.

16. Letters of Striggio to Aurelio Zibramonte, Mantua, 11, 12 November 1574, in ASMN, AG 2593. Striggio also wrote from Mantua to Francesco de' Medici in Florence on 11 November 1574: in ASF, Mediceo del principato 666, fol. 118.

17. In ASF, Mediceo del principato 616, fol. 376v.

18. David S. Butchart, "The Festive Madrigals of Alessandro Striggio," *Proceedings of the Royal Musical Association* 107 (1980–81): 51–52.

19. See Ghisi, *Feste musicali*, pp. xxxv–xl; Leo Schrade, "The Festivities at the Wedding of Francesco dei Medici and Bianca Cappello," in Leo Schrade, *De scientia musicae studia atque orationes* (Bern-Stuttgart: Heide/Holst, 1967), pp. 325–59 (originally in French in *Les fêtes de la renaissance*, vol. 1, ed. Jean Jacquot [Paris: Éditions du Centre National de la Recherche Scientifique, 1956], pp. 107–31); and Butchart, "The Festive Madrigals," pp. 53–54.

20. Ghisi, *Feste musicali*, pp. xl–xli.

21. Ibid., pp. xlii-xlvi; see also Brown, *Sixteenth-Century Instrumentation*, pp. 105-7.

22. The fullest account of this is in Anthony Newcomb, *The Madrigal at Ferrara, 1579–1597* (Princeton: Princeton University Press, 1980), 1:53ff. Striggio's letters are reprinted in Riccardo Gandolfi, "Lettere inedite scritte da musicisti e letterati . . . ," *Rivista musicale italiana* 20 (1913): 528ff.

23. See letter of Striggio to Francesco de' Medici, Mantua, 20 April 1585, in ASF, Mediceo del principato 772, fol. 630; and Gandolfi, "Lettere inedite," p. 536 (with reference to ASF, Mediceo del principato 770, however). The letters concerning Strig-

gio's commission from Grand Duchess Bianca Cappello are reprinted in Warren Kirkendale, "Alessandro Striggio und die Medici: neue Briefe und Dokumente," in *Festschrift O. Wessely zum 80. Geburtstag* (Tutzing: Schneider, 1982), pp. 335–39.

24. See letter of Striggio to Federico Cattaneo, Mantua, 17 August 1586, in ASMN, AG 2636, fol. 709v. Striggo's final departure is recorded in Agostino Lapini, *Diario fiorentino dal 252 al 1596*, ed. G. O. Corazzini (Florence: Sansoni, 1900), p. 258.

25. Letter of Striggio to Francesco de' Medici, Mantua, 3 September 1587, in ASF, Mediceo del principato 789, fol. 30; see Gandolfi, "Lettere inedite," pp. 537–38.

26. *Intermedi et concerti . . .* (Venice: Giacomo Vincenti, 1591; RISM 1591⁷), *nono* partbook, notes to fifth *intermedio*.

27. ASMN, AG 395, fasc. xii, *Affari diversi della corte*, fol. 159v.

28. The plaque is in Mantua in the Church of Santa Maria della Carità.

29. ASMN, AG, *Registro necrologico* 19 (1591–92), fol. 108v. The entry reads: "Sabbato a 29 di Febraro 1592. Il signor Alessandro Striggio nella contrata cervo è morto di febre in quindeci dì d'anni Numero 55 [abbreviated forms expanded]."

30. The precise details surrounding the publication of these collections are not clear. See Richard J. Agee, "The Venetian Privilege and Music-Printing in the Sixteenth Century," *Early Music History* 3 (Cambridge: Cambridge University Press, 1983): 40, for the concession of a privilege on these books—dated 17 June 1597. However, by 1597, the *Terzo libro* and *Quarto libro* had long been printed (their letters of dedication bear the dates 10 and 26 September 1596, respectively). Further documentation in Richard J. Agee, "The Privilege and Venetian Music Printing in the Sixteenth Century" (Ph.D. diss., Princeton University, 1982), pp. 325–28, covering the period 27 April to 4 May 1597, indicates that the authorities seem to have examined only the *Terzo libro* and *Quarto libro*, although the manuscript (or, possibly, print) they received was entitled "Il terzo quarto e quinto libro de madrigali a cinque voci." This volume consisted of ten folios (*carte*) whose first madrigal was *All'hor che lieta* (= *Terzo libro*, No. 1) and whose final madrigal ended "un bel rubore" (= last line, final madrigal, *Quarto libro*). The list of contents would therefore seem to confirm the "separation" of the *Terzo libro* and *Quarto libro* from the *Quinto libro*, but it does not allow us to establish an exact sequence of events in the publishing history of all three books.

31. Two poets, Giovanbattista Strozzi, senior, and Cesare Rinaldi, wrote verses praising Striggio's instrumental virtuosity above all. In prose, Striggio was esteemed by Sansovino and Bartoli (see n. 7 above) as well as by Torquato Tasso, Vincenzo Galilei, and Thomaso Garzoni.

32. Eugenio Cagnani, *Raccolta d'alcune rime di scrittori mantovani con una lettera cronologica . . .* (Mantua: Osanna, 1612), p. 17.

33. Giovanbattista Doni, *Compendio del trattato de'generi e de'modi della musica . . .* (Rome: Fei, 1635), p. 117.

34. Charles Burney, *A General History of Music* (London: printed for the author, 1789), 3:244.

35. François-Joseph Fétis, *Biographie universelle . . . supplément et complément publiés sous la direction de M. Arthur Pougin* (Paris: Firmin-Didot, 1878), 1:159.

36. Angelo Solerti and Domenico Alaleona, "Primi saggi del melodramma giocoso," *Rivista musicale italiana* 12 (1905): 814–38.

37. Einstein, *The Italian Madrigal*, 2:761–68.

38. Butchart, "The Festive Madrigals," pp. 55–56.

39. Einstein, *The Italian Madrigal*, 2:760–61.

40. Butchart, "The First Published Compositions," p. 36.

41. See Donna G. Cardamone, "The Debut of the Canzone Villanesca alla Napolitana," *Studi musicali* 4 (1975): 65–130.

42. See the comments of Einstein, *The Italian Madrigal*, 2:760–61 and 766, on the *Cicalamento*.

43. Don Harrán, "Rore and the *Madrigale cromatico*," *The Music Review* 34 (1973): 66–81.

44. Einstein, *The Italian Madrigal*, 2:764.

45. The single exception is the *seconda parte* of *O messagi del cor* (No. [12]), where he adopted the *misura comune* (C), and where the harmonic rhythm increases noticeably; a slower tempo is probably appropriate. For discussion of the differences between *misura di breve* and *misura comune* (and the confusion arising therefrom), see James Haar, "The *Note Nere* Madrigal," *Journal of the American Musicological Society* 18 (1965): 22–41.

46. Einstein, *The Italian Madrigal*, 1:404.

47. Ibid., 2:764.

48. Ray J. Tadlock, "Alessandro Striggio, Madrigalist," *Journal of the American Musicological Society* 11 (1958): 39.

49. Pirrotta, *Li due Orfei*, pp. 216, 264 (n. 65).

50. Einstein, *The Italian Madrigal*, 2:764.

51. Pirrotta, *Li due Orfei*, p. 264 (translation from English ed., *Music and Theatre*, p. 194, n. 67).

52. See *The New Grove Dictionary of Music and Musicians*, s.v. "Chiavette," by Siegfried Hermelink.

53. Butchart, "A Musical Journey," p. 3.

54. As described in Anton Francesco Doni, *Dialogo della musica* (Venice: Scotto, 1544), dedicatory letter in the tenor part.

55. Brown, *Sixteenth-Century Instrumentation*, pp. 96–105.

Texts, Translations, and Critical Commentary

In this section, the Critical Commentary follows the presentation of the text and translation for each madrigal. In the commentary on the text, citations of the author and source of the poetry are made, and any explanatory notes on text content are given. In the case of texts by Petrarch, the principal edition referred to for the standardization of orthography (see The Edition) is Francesco Petrarca, *Le rime sparse e i trionfe*, ed. Ezio Chiorboli (Bari: Laterza, 1930). Where necessary, there are notes on textual variations and notes on any changes made to the text by the present editor.

Commentary on the music follows commentary on the text. Relevant information on sources (cited by the *sigla* explained in the Sources section) is given in the following order: manuscript versions (listed chronologically); madrigal anthologies; printed arrangements; and modern editions. Note that while concordant manuscripts for *Il primo libro . . . a sei voci* are listed individually as appropriate, the concordant prints are not cited again in the Critical Commentary, because it is understood that each print contains the entire collection (with the exception of the *aggiunti*). Discrepancies between the 1565 print (the primary source) and this edition are then cited and, unless otherwise indicated, all references are to this source in the Critical Commentary. "M" is the abbreviation for "measure," and pitches are given according to the familiar method, wherein c′ = middle C, c″ = the C above middle C, and so forth.

[1] I dolci colli ov'io lasciai me stesso

Prima parte
I dolci colli ov'io lasciai me stesso,
Partendo, onde partir già mai non posso,
Mi vanno innanzi, et emmi ogn'hor adosso
Quel caro peso ch'Amor m'ha commesso.

Meco di me mi meraviglio spesso,
Ch'i' pur vo sempr'e non son anchor mosso
Dal bel giogo più volt'indarno scosso,
Ma com' più me n'allungo et più m'appresso.

Seconda parte
Et qual cervo ferito di saetta

Col ferro avellenato dentr'al fianco
Fugge, et più duolsi quanto più s'affretta,

Tal'io con quello stral dal lato manco,
Che mi consuma et parte mi diletta,
Di duol mi struggo et di fuggir mi stanco.

(The gentle hills, where I left myself behind
On parting, so I can never really depart,
Come before me; and I carry forever
That precious burden which Love has entrusted to me.

Thinking of myself, I am often amazed
That I still go on and am not yet released
From the easy yoke which I have often tried to shake off
But the more I draw away, the more attached I become.

Just as the deer, wounded by an arrow,
With the poisonous tip in its side
Flees, and suffers the more it hurries,

So do I, with that arrow in my heart;
It wears me out, and at the same time brings me pleasure;
I languish in pain, and grow weary of flight.)

Critical Commentary

TEXT
Sonnet. Francesco Petrarca, *Canzoniere*, CCIX.
The hills are those of Provence, where the poet first encountered Laura, in the Church of Saint Clair in Avignon, on 6 April (Good Friday) 1327.

MUSIC
MS Versions—(1) RegB 775, Nos. 16–17.
Printed Arrangements—(1) Vincenzo Galilei, *Fronimo dialogo . . . nel quale si contengono le vere et necessarie regole del intavolare la musica nel liuto* (Venice: Girolamo Scotto, 1568), No. 87, pp. 151–52. (2) Gabriel Fallamero, *Il primo libro de intavolatura da liuto . . .* (Venice: Erede di Girolamo Scotto, 1584), No. 43, pp. 72–74; RISM 1584[13]. (3) Girolamo Dalla Casa, *Il vero modo di diminuir, con tutte le sorte di stromenti di fiato, et corda, et di voce humana . . . libro primo* (Venice: Angelo Gardano, 1584), No. 7, p. 14.
Variants—M. 144, canto, note 3 is f′-sharp in 1560. M. 179, quinto, note 1 is half-note.

[2] Nasce la pena mia

Nasce la pena mia,
Non potendo mirar mio vivo sole;
E la mia vita è ria
Qual hor lo miro, perch'il guard'è tale,
Che lasciarmi peggior che morte suole.
Ahi, vita trista e frale,
Che fia dunque di me, che farmi deggio?
S'io mir'ho male, e s'io non mir'ho peggio.

(My torment begins
When I cannot gaze upon my dazzling sun;
And my life is wretched
Whenever I admire it, for its glance is so strong
That it usually leaves me worse off than death.
Ah, sad, feeble life,
What will become of me then, what should I do?
If I gaze, I feel pain; and if I don't, I feel worse.)

Critical Commentary

TEXT

Madrigal. Author unidentified.

The text forms the first half of a madrigal pair, first set complete by Hoste da Reggio (*maestro di cappella*, between 1548 and 1553, to the Governor of Milan, Ferrante Gonzaga) in his *Secondo libro delli madrigali a quattro voce* (Venice: Girolamo Scotto, 1554). The first half of this setting is also included in da Reggio's *Primo libro de madrigali a tre voci* (Milan: Francesco and Simone Moscheni, 1554). The second half is entitled *Nasce la gioia mia*: it has a metrical and rhyme scheme identical to *Nasce la pena mia* (aBaCBcDD; with lowercase letters indicating seven-syllable and uppercase letters indicating eleven-syllable lines.

MUSIC

MS Versions—(1) ModE C311, No. 93, fols. 39v–40r. (2) FlorML 641, fols. 25v–28v. (3) WroU 51435, unfoliated. (4) WroU 51335, unfoliated. (5) RegB 775, No. 18. (6) WarU Olkuz, fols. 4–5; contrafactum, *Dilagam te Domine fortitudo mea.* (7) TübU 40034, fol. 28r. (8) ParBN 851, pp. 244–45 (no. 235). (9) MilBC Tarasconi, fol. 166v (no. 194). (10) CraJ 40032, fols. 30v–31r. (11) BruCR 27089, fols. 156v–58r; Monte's six-part parody mass follows (to fol. 180r). (12) BolC C33, fols. 37v–38r [corrected foliation]; partially reproduced in Richard Erig and Veronika Gutmann, *Italienische Diminutionen* (Zurich: Päuler, 1979), p. 47; see Modern Editions, below. (13) LonBL 30491, fol. 48v, as "Nasce la pena mia di Gio[vanni] Macque"; in contents list of MS (fol. 52v) as "Nasce la pena mia passeggiato da Fran[ces]co Lambardi"; the diminution arrangement is based on Striggio's setting; see Modern Editions, below. (14) UtrR Lerma, fols. 147v–48r. (15) BolC Q34, fols. 60v–63r. (16) PelpS 305, fols. 45v–46r (derived from contrafactum, *Dilagam te Domine*); the Kyrie of an anonymous eight-part parody mass appears in MS 306, fols. 102v–7r. (17) MunBS 218, No. 29, p. 70. (18) UppU 409, fols. 49v–50r. (19) (?) LegT 20, No. 62. (20) (?) LegT 24, No. 46. (21) The Königliche Hausbibliothek, Berlin (now Staatsbibliothek Preussicher Kulturbesitz) formerly held a manuscript (Mus. MS 40.028, *olim* Z 28) that contained a contrafactum of *Nasce la pena mia*, entitled *Faciem tuam Deum*, apparently derived from *Gemma musicalis. . . . Libro primo* (Nuremberg: C. Gerlach, 1588); the MS was in score and dated 1599; Striggio's piece was at fol. 37; the MS is no longer to be found at the Staatsbibliothek, and its present location is uncertain.

Madrigal Anthologies—(1) *Harmonia celeste di diversi eccellentissimi musici a IIII. V. VI. VII. et VIII. voci, nuovamente raccolta per Andrea Pevernage . . .* (Antwerp: Pierre Phalèse and Jacques Bellère, 1583); RISM 1583[14]. (2) *Gemma musicalis: selectissimas stili cantiones (vulgo Italis madrigali et napolitane dicuntur) quatuor, quinque, sex et plurimum vocum continens . . . studio et opera Friderici Lindneri lignicensis. Liber primus* (Nuremberg: C. Gerlach, 1588); RISM 1588[21].

Printed Arrangements—(1) Antonio di Becchi, *Libro primo d'intabulatura da leuto* (Venice: Girolamo Scotto, 1568), No. 29, p. 66. (2) Vincenzo Galilei, *Fronimo dialogo . . . nel quale si contengono le vere et necessarie regole del intavolare la musica nel liuto* (Venice: Girolamo Scotto, 1568), No. 6, p. 24; on p. 92, No. 44: "Fantasia Prima. Sopra Nasce la pena mia." Cf. Idem, *Fronimo dialogo . . . nuovamente ristampato, et dall'autore istesso arrichito* (Venice: Erede di Girolamo Scotto, 1584), No. 13, fol. 44; RISM 1584[15] (= 1568 ed., No. 6, p. 24). (3) Lodovico Agostino, *L'echo et enigmi musicali a sei voci* (Venice: Alessandro Gardano, 1581), pp. 14–18: "Canzone a imitaz. di Nasce la pena di Striggio" (5 sections); RISM 1581[5]. (4) Jakob Paix, *Ein schön nutz unnd gebreüchlich Orgel Tablaturbuch* (Laugingen: Leonhart Reinmichel, 1583), No. 31, fol. 99; RISM 1583[23]; German keyboard tablature. (5) Emanuel Adriansen, *Pratum musicum . . .* (Antwerp: Pierre Phalèse, 1584), No. 31, fol. 37v; RISM 1584[12]; arrangement for lute and voices (canto, basso). (6) Gabriel Fallamero, *Il primo libro de intabulatura da liuto . . .* (Venice: Erede di Girolamo Scotto, 1584), No. 45, p. 77. (7) Girolamo Dalla Casa, *Il vero modo di diminuir . . . libro primo* (Venice: Angelo Gardano, 1584), No. 6, p. 13; reproduced in Richard Erig and Veronika Gutmann, *Italienische Diminutionen* (Zurich: Päuler, 1979), p. 23; see Modern Editions, below. (8) Giovanni Bassano, *Motetti, madrigali et canzoni francese di diversi eccellentissimi auttori a quattro, cinque, et sei voci. Diminuiti per sonar con ogni sorte di stromenti, et anco per cantar a semplice voce* (Venice: Giacomo Vincenti, 1591), No. 39, p. 56; see Modern Editions, below. (9) Thomas Mancinus, *Duum vocum cantiuncularum* (Helmstadt: Jacobus Lucius, 1597), No. 1, fol. A2v; two partbooks, mensural notation. (10) Giovanni Antonio Terzi, *Il secondo libro de intavolatura di liuto . . .* (Venice: Giacomo Vincenti, 1599), No. 16,

p. 18, ". . con passaggi . . ."; RISM 1599[19]. (11) Bernhard Schmid, *Tablatur Buch von allerhand ausserlesnen, schönen, lieblichen Praeludijs, Toccaten, Motteten, Canzonetten, Madrigalien unnd Fugen von 4. 5. und 6. Stimmen . . .* (Strasbourg: Lazarus Zetzner, 1607), No. 61; RISM 1607[29]. (12) Michael Herrer, *Hortus musicalis, variis antea diversorum authorum Italiae floribus consitus, jam vero latinos fructus . . . liber secundus* (Munich: A. Berg, 1609); RISM 1609[14]; a contrafactum (*Nascitur cum dolore*).

Modern Editions—(1) Philippe de Monte, *Opera: Missa Nasce la pena mia*, ed. Charles Van den Borren and Julius Van Nuffel (Düsseldorf, 1929; reprint, Broude Bros.: New York, 1965), Vol. 10, supplement pp. 1–10. (2) Cosimo Bottegari, *The Bottegari Lutebook*, ed. Carol MacClintock (Wellesley, Mass.: Broude Bros., 1965), No. 93, pp. 120–23; for voice and lute. (3) Richard Erig and Veronika Gutmann, *Italienische Diminutionen* (Zürich: Päuler, 1979), pp. 291–305, with BolC C33, LonBL 30491, Dalla Casa, and Bassano arrangements.

[3] Anchor ch'io possa dire

Anchor ch'io possa dire,
Che d'haver vita il cor soltanto sente
Quant'a voi son presente;
Poi che non m'è concesso
Esservi ogn'hor appresso,
Mai non vorrei venire,
Mia vita, innanzi a voi,
Tant'ho dolor de la partita poi.

(Although I can say
That my heart only feels alive
As long as I am with you,
Since I am not allowed
To be with you all the time,
I would never wish to come,
My life, into your presence,
Such is the pain I suffer when I leave afterwards.)

Critical Commentary

Text

Madrigal. Girolamo Parabosco, *Rime di M. Girolamo Parabosco* (Venice: Antonio Gardano, 1547), p. 17v.

A *risposta* to *Anchor che col partire* (attrib. to Alfonso D'Avalos), made famous in a madrigal setting by Rore, first published in Perissone Cambio, *Il primo libro de madrigali a quatro voci* (Venice: Antonio Gardano, 1547), No. 31, pp. 27–28; RISM 1547[14]. See No. [20] of the present edition for Cambio's setting of the text set also by Rore, *Anchor che col partire*.

Music

MS Versions—(1) FlorBN LF2, No. 15, fols. 14v–15r. (2) RegB 775, No. 19. (3) ParBN 851, p. 245 (no. 236). (4) MilBC Tarasconi, fol. 165v (no. 193). (5) UtrR Lerma, fols. 158v–59r.

Madrigal Anthologies—(1) *Melodia olympica di diversi eccellentissimi musici a IIII. V. VI. et VIII voci, nuovamente raccolta da Pietro Phillippi inglese . . .* (Antwerp: Pierre Phalèse and Jacques Bellère, 1591), No. 44, p. 30v; RISM 1591[10].

Printed Arrangements—(1) Vincenzo Galilei, *Fronimo dialogo . . . nel quale si contengono le vere et necessarie regole del intavolare la musica nel liuto* (Venice: Girolamo Scotto, 1568), No. 89, p. 153. (2) Gabriel Fallamero, *Il primo libro de intavolatura da liuto . . .* (Venice: Erede di Girolamo Scotto, 1584), No. 44, p. 75. (3) Girolamo Dalla Casa, *Il vero modo di diminuir . . . libro primo* (Venice: Angelo Gardano, 1584), No. 30, p. 39; see Modern Edition, below. (4) Giovanni Bassano, *Motetti, madrigali et canzoni francese . . . diminuiti* (Venice: Giacomo Vincenti, 1591), No. 40, p. 58; see Modern Edition, below. (5) Giovanni Antonio Terzi, *Intavolatura di liutto, accomodata con diversi passagi per suonar in concerti a duoi liutti et solo. Libro primo* (Venice: Riccardo Amadino, 1593), No. 12, p. 34; RISM 1593[11]; on p. 35 "Contraponto sopra Anchor ch'io . . . a l'unisono per suonar a doi liutti, et in concerto"; p. 35 reproduced in Richard Erig and Veronika Gutmann, *Italienische Diminutionen* (Zürich: Päuler, 1979), p. 45; see Modern Edition, below.

Modern Edition—(1) Richard Erig and Veronika Gutmann, *Italienische Diminutionen* (Zürich: Päuler, 1979), pp. 211–23, with Dalla Casa, Bassano, and Terzi arrangements.

[4] Lasciat'hai, Morte, senza sol il mondo

Prima parte
Lasciat'hai, Morte, senza sol il mondo
Oscuro et freddo, Amor cieco et inerme,
Legiadria ignuda, le bellezze inferme,
Me sconsolato et a me grave pondo,

Cortesia in band'et honestate in fondo;
Dogliom'io sol, né sol'ho da dolerme,
Ché svelt'hai di virtut'il chiaro germe:
Spent'il primo valor, qual fia 'l secondo?

Seconda parte
Pianger l'aere et la terra e 'l mar devrebbe
L'human legnagio, che senz'ella è quasi
Senza fior prato, o senza gemm'anello.

Non la conobbe il mondo mentre l'hebbe:
Conobbil'io, ch'a pianger qui rimasi,
E 'l ciel, che del mio piant'hor si fa bello.

(Death, you have left the world without a sun,
Dark and cold; Love, blind and disarmed;
Gracefulness, destitute; beauty, ailing;
I myself, disheartened and weighed down in thought;

Courtesy, set aside; integrity, debased;
I am alone in my sorrow, yet not only I have cause to
   lament,

For you have rooted out the bright seed of virtue:
With the chief virtue gone, what will become of the
   second?

The air and the earth and the sea should weep for
The race of men that, without her, is like
A meadow without a flower, or a ring without a jewel.

The world did not appreciate her while it had her;
I, who am left here to weep, loved her,
As did the heavens, now graced with my lament.)

Critical Commentary

TEXT

Sonnet. Francesco Petrarca, *Canzoniere*, CCCXXXVIII.
Line 2—"inherme" in 1565.

MUSIC

MS Versions—(1) RegB 775, Nos. 20–21. (2) MilBC
Tarasconi, fol. 167v (no. 195). (3) (?) LegT 31, p. 110.
Variants—M. 86, tenore, note 2 is f-sharp in 1578.

[5] Madonna, poich'occidermi volete

Madonna, poich'occidermi volete,
Non nego di morire;
Ma se con dolci sguardi voi potete
La mia vita finire,
Non è più giusta voglia
Ch'io muoia di dolcezza che di doglia?

(Lady, since you want to kill me,
I do not refuse to die;
But if with tender looks you can
End my life,
Is it not a more just desire
That I die of pleasure rather than of pain?)

Critical Commentary

TEXT

Madrigal. Author unidentified.
In connection with a setting by Giaches de Wert
(*Primo libro de madrigali a quattro voci*, 1561), Einstein,
The Italian Madrigal, 2:517, calls this "an old-fashioned
text in the style of Cassola." It was popular in madrigal
settings throughout the sixteenth century.

MUSIC

MS Versions—(1) RegB 775, No. 22.

[6] Se ben di sette stell'ardent'e belle

Prima parte
Se ben di sette stell'ardent'e belle
Ti cinge il biondo crin lieta corona,
Mentr'a diport'in queste part'e 'n quelle
Vai con la vaga figlia di Latona,
Pur t'acceser'il cor l'empie facelle
Del fier arcier di Gnido, onde ne suona

Il lido anchora, e l'arenosa sponda,
Che 'l mar di Creta mormorand'innonda.

Seconda parte
Fosti amante com'io, com'io piangesti
Lagrime di dolor cald'et amare,
E con accenti dolorosi e mesti
Facesti col tuo duol pietoso il mare;
Teco voglio parlar, teco, e con questi
Duri lamenti miei voglio sfogare
L'interna pena, ch'ogni pena avanza
Per la mia lung'e dura lontananza.

(Although a luminous crown of seven stars,
Blazing and beautiful, wreathes your fair hair,
As you go strolling here and there
With the lovely daughter of Latona,
The pitiless darts of Cnido's fierce archer
Still inflamed your heart, whence resounds
Once more the shore and sandy bank
Which the Cretan sea murmuringly floods.

Were you as loving as I am, like me you would weep
Bitter, passionate tears of sorrow,
And with doleful, dejected tones
You would make the sea pity you in your sorrow;
With you I long to speak, with you; and with these
Bitter complaints of mine, I wish to give vent
To the inner torment which exceeds all other pain
During my long and trying absence from you.)

Critical Commentary

TEXT

Two *ottava rima* stanzas. Bernardo Tasso, *Stanze di
Lontananza*, 1–2; in Andrea Arrivabene (compiler), *Libro
terzo de le rime di diversi noblissimi et eccellentissimi
autori nuovamente raccolte* (Venice: A. Aiolito de' ferrari,
1550), p. 60v.

The version in Tasso's revised edition of his *Rime*
(Venice: Al segno del pozzo, 1560), p. 18, differs at several
points from Striggio's underlaid (1565) text. The
1560 Tasso edition has the following variants : line 1,
"nove" for "sette"; line 7, "Ancor il lido"; line 9,
"spargesti" for "piangesti"; line 12, "del" for "col";
line 16, "De" for "per." Striggio's underlaid (1565) text
omits an emphasizing "io," line 13; both 1561 and 1563
versions have "voglio io."

Line 1—"sette stell[e]" = the Moon, Mercury, Venus,
the Sun, Mars, Jupiter, Saturn (i.e., the "stars"
known to astronomers of the time). Perhaps, too, a reference
to the seven virtues (four cardinal, three theological).
Line 4—"figlia di Latona" = Diana, goddess of
hunting, of the moon, and a symbol of chastity. Line
6—"fier arcier di Gnido" = Eros (Cupid), son of
Aphrodite (Venus). He is frequently depicted with
bow and arrow, in the act of launching his darts,
which inflame human hearts with amorous passion.
Gnido was an ancient Greek city in southwest Asia Mi-

nor (Turkey). Its most famous sanctuary was dedicated to Aphrodite, goddess of love.

MUSIC

MS Versions—(1) FlorBN LF2, fols. 16v–17r. (2) RegB 775, No. 25. (3) MilBC Tarasconi, fol. 181v (no. 198). (4) (?) LegT 31, p. 113.

Variants—Mm. 182–83, sesto, notes are b in 1560 and 1565, and a in 1578 and 1579; all other sources have d.

[7] Quando vede 'l pastor calar i raggi

Quando vede 'l pastor calar i raggi
Del gran pianeta al nid'ov'egli alberga,
E 'mbrunir le contrade d'oriente,
Drizzas'in piedi, et con l'usata verga,
Lassando l'herba et le fontan'e i faggi,
Move la schiera sua soavemente;
Poi lontan da la gente
O casetta o spelunca
Di verdi frond'ingiunca:
Ivi senza pensier s'adagia et dorme.
Ahi, crud'Amor, m'al'hor tu più m'informe
A seguir d'una fera che mi strugge
La voce e i passi et l'orme,
Et lei non stringi che s'appiatt'et fugge.

(When the shepherd sees the rays
Of the sun sink down into the west where he dwells,
And the realms of the east darken,
He gets to his feet, and, taking his well-worn staff,
He leaves the pasture, the springs, and the beech-
grove,
And slowly leads off his flock;
Then, far from human kind,
He strews with green rushes
A little hut or cavern:
There, without a worry, he settles down and sleeps.
Ah, cruel Love, then it is you goad me the more
To pursue a wild animal who wears out
My voice, my stride, and my tracks,
And you do not hold her back, as she crouches and
flees.)

Critical Commentary

TEXT

Canzone stanza. Francesco Petrarca, *Canzoniere*, L; stanza 3, lines 29–42, of *Ne la stagion che 'l ciel rapido inchina.*

Line 11—"Ah crud'Amor, ma tu allhor più m'informe" in Petrarca, *Canzoniere.*

MUSIC

MS Version—(1) RegB 775, No. 24.

Printed Arrangement—(1) Vincenzo Galilei, *Fronimo dialogo . . . nel quale si contengono le vere et necessarie regole del intavolare la musica nel liuto* (Venice: Girolamo Scotto, 1568), No. 91, p. 155.

[8] Voglia mi sprona, Amor mi guid'e scorge

Voglia mi sprona, Amor mi guid'e scorge,
Piacer mi tira, usanza mi trasporta,
Speranza mi lusinga et riconforta,
Et la man destr'al cor già stanco porge.

Il misero la prende et non s'accorge
Di nostra cieca et disleale scorta;
Regnan'i sensi, et la ragion è morta;
De l'un vago desio l'altro risorge.

(Desire incites me, Love leads and directs me,
Pleasure attracts me, habit carries me on,
Hope flatters and entices me
And holds out his right hand to my already weary
heart.

The wretch accepts it, and remains unaware
Of our blind, dishonest guide;
The senses prevail, and reason is dead;
One fickle desire gives rise to another.)

Critical Commentary

TEXT

Sonnet octave. Francesco Petrarca, *Canzoniere*, CCXI.

MUSIC

MS Versions—(1) RegB 775, No. 27. (2) UtrR Lerma, fols. 149v–50r.

Printed Arrangement—(1) Vincenzo Galilei, *Fronimo dialogo . . . nel quale si contengono le vere et necessarie regole del intavolare la musica nel liuto* (Venice: Girolamo Scotto, 1568), No. 93, p. 157.

Variants—M. 60, quinto has redundant half-rest.

[9] Là ver l'aurora che sì dolce l'aura

Là ver l'aurora che sì dolce l'aura
Al tempo nuovo suol mover i fiori
Et gl'augeletti incominciar lor versi,
Sì dolcemente i pensier dentr'a l'alma
Mover mi sento a chi gl'ha tutt'in forza,
Che ritornar conviemm'a le mie note.

(Just as day breaks, when the breeze so gently
Stirs the flowers, as it is wont in springtime,
And the little birds take up their songs,
So gently do I feel the thoughts within my soul
Bestirred by the one who holds them in her complete
power
That I feel compelled to go back to my verses.)

Critical Commentary

TEXT

Sestina stanza. Francesco Petrarca, *Canzoniere*, CCXXXIX; stanza 1, lines 1–6.

Line 2—"muover" in 1565 print.

Music

MS Versions—(1) MilBC Tarasconi, fol. 179v (no. 196). (2) UtrR Lerma, fols. 150v–51r. (3) BolC Q34, fols. 63r–65r. (4) (?) LegT 31, p. 94.

Madrigal Anthology—(1) *Melodia olympica . . .* (Antwerp: Phalèse and Bellère, 1591), No. 42, p. 28r.

Printed Arrangements—(1) Vincenzo Galilei, *Fronimo dialogo . . . nel quale si contengono le vere et necessarie regole del intavolare la musica nel liuto* (Venice: Girolamo Scotto, 1568), No. 90, p. 154. (2) Girolamo Dalla Casa, *Il vero modo di diminuir . . . libro primo* (Venice: Angelo Gardano, 1584), No. 12, p. 16.

[10] Che fai? che pensi? che pur dietro guardi

Che fai? che pensi? che pur dietro guardi
Nel tempo che tornar non pote homai,
Anima sconsolata? che pur vai
Giugnendo legn'al foco ove tu ardi?

Le soavi parole e i dolci sguardi,
Ch'ad un ad un descritti et dipint'hai,
Son levati da terra; et è, ben sai,
Qui ricercarli intempestivo et tardi.

(What are you doing? What are you thinking of? What
   are you still looking back for,
To the time which cannot ever return,
Dejected soul? What wood are you still
Adding to the fire where it is you who burn?

The tender words and the gentle looks
Which, one by one, you have described and depicted,
Are removed from the earth, and, you know well, it is
Inopportune and late to look for them here.)

Critical Commentary

Text

Sonnet octave. Francesco Petrarca, *Canzoniere,* CCLXXIII.

Music

MS Version—(1)(?) LegT 31, p. 93.

[11] Amor, io fallo, e veggio 'l mio fallire

Prima parte

Amor, io fallo, e veggio 'l mio fallire,
Ma fo sì com'huom ch'arde e 'l fuoc'ha 'n seno,
Ché 'l duol pur cresce, e la ragion vien meno
Et è già quasi vinta dal martire.

Solea frenar il mio caldo desire,
Per non turbar il bel viso sereno:
Non posso più, di man m'hai tolto il freno
E l'alma disperando ha pres'ardire.

Seconda parte
Però, s'oltra suo stil'ella s'aventa,
Tu 'l fai, che sì l'accendi e sì la sproni,
Ch'ogn'aspra via per sua salute tenta;

E più 'l fanno i celesti e rari doni
C'ha in sé madonna. Hor fa almen ch'ella 'l senta,
E le mie colpe a se stessa perdoni.

(I am at fault, Love, and I see my fault,
But act just like a man who rages with fire in his chest,
For the pain still grows, and reason prevails less,
And is almost overcome by the torment already.

I usually reined in my passionate desire,
So as not to disturb her fine, calm air;
I cannot do so any longer; you have seized the rein
   from my hand,
And the soul, in desperation, has taken courage.

Therefore, if it risks more than it is wont,
It is you who make it, by exciting and goading it so
That it tries every rough road to save itself;

And still more are the cause the divine, rare virtues
Which madonna has in herself. Now, at least make her
   aware,
And pardon herself for my faults.)

Critical Commentary

Text

Sonnet. Francesco Petrarca, *Canzoniere,* CCXXXVI.

Music

MS Versions—(1) MilBC Tarasconi, fol. 183v (no. 199). (2) UtrR Lerma, fols. 151v–52r (*seconda parte* only). (3) (?) LegT 31, p. 115.

[12] O messagi del cor, sospiri ardenti

Prima parte
O messagi del cor, sospiri ardenti,
O lagrime ch'el giorn'io celo a pena,
O preghi sparsi in non fecond'arena,
O del mio ingiusto mal giusti lamenti,

O sempr'in un voler pensier intenti,
O desir che ragion mai non raffrena,
O speranze ch'Amor dietro si mena,
Quand'a gran salti e quand'a passi lenti:

Seconda parte
Sarà che cessi o che s'allenti mai
Vostro lungo travaglio e 'l mio martire,
O pur fia l'un'e l'altr'insiem'eterno?

Che fia non so, ma ben chiaro discerno
Ch'el mio poco consiglio e 'l tropp'ardire
Soli poss'incolpar ch'io viv'in guai.

(O messages of the heart, you ardent sighs,
O tears which I just manage to hide by day,
O entreaties cast on barren ground,
O righteous laments of my undeserved pain,

O thoughts ever intent on one desire,
O desire which reason never restrains,
O hopes which Love carries along,

Sometimes with great leaps, sometimes with slow
   steps:

Will your long distress ever cease,
Or my torment ever diminish,
Or are the one and the other indeed bound forever?

What will be I do not know, but I see quite clearly
That I can blame my weak reason and excessive
   passion
Alone for my life of woe.)

Critical Commentary

Text

   Sonnet. Lodovico Ariosto, in *Lirica*, ed. Giuseppe Fatini (Bari: Laterza, 1924), p. 39.

   The first edition of Ariosto's *Rime* (Venice: Jacopo Modanese, 1546) included this sonnet. Its quatrain scheme (the series of vocatives) derives from Petrarch's *O passi sparsi, o pensier vaghi e pronti, Canzoniere,* CLXI (later set by Striggio, and included in the anthology *Musica di diversi auttori illustri per cantar et sonar in concerti . . .* (Venice: Giacomo Vincenti and Riccardo Amadino, 1584; RISM 1584[4]).

Music

   MS Versions—(1) UtrR Lerma, fols. 148–49r (*seconda parte* only). (2) (?) LegT 31, p. 116.

   Variants—Mm. 82–84, basso, no text underlay present; all other editions consulted have *ij.*

[13] Poi che spiegat'ho l'ale al bel desio

Prima parte
Poi che spiegat'ho l'ale al bel desio,
Quanto più sotto 'l pié l'aria mi scorgo,
Più le superbe penne al vento porgo,
E spreggio 'l mond', e verso 'l ciel m'invio.

Né del figliuol di Dedalo il fin rio
Fa che giù pieghi, anzi via più risorgo:
Ch'io cadrò mort'a terra ben m'accorgo;
Ma qual vita pareggia 'l morir mio?

Seconda parte
La voce del mio cor per l'aria sento:
Ove mi porti, temerario? china,
Ché rar'è senza duol tropp'ardimento.

Non temer, rispond'io, l'alta ruina;
Fendi secur le nub'e muor contento,
Se 'l ciel s'illustre morte ne destina.

(Since I spread my wings toward fair desire,
The more I sense the air beneath my feet,
The more I stretch my proud feathers to the wind,
And, disdaining the world, direct myself towards
   the heavens.

Nor does the cruel fate of Dedalus's son
Make me turn back down; rather I rise up all the more.

I realize well that I will fall dead to earth,
But what life is equal to this death of mine?

I hear my heart's voice in the air:
Where are you taking me, rash one? Go down,
For rare is the passion that does not suffer.

Do not be afraid of a noble death, I reply;
Cleave the clouds with confidence, and die content,
If the heavens assign you so illustrious an end.)

Critical Commentary

Text

   Sonnet. Luigi Tansillo, in Lodovico Dolce (compiler), *Rime di diversi illustri signori napoletani . . .* (Venice: A. Aiolito de ferrari et fratelli, 1552), p. 6.

   The standard modern edition of Tansillo's poetry, Erasmo Pèrcopo, ed., *Luigi Tansillo. Il canzoniere edito ed inedito* (Naples: Tipografia degli Artigianelli, S. Raffaele, 1926), 1:5, differs considerably at several points: line 2—"Quanto per l'alte nubi altier lo scorgo"; line 4—"E, d'ardir colmo, verso il ciel l'invio"; line 6—"Fa ch'io paventi"; line 8—"s'agguaglia" for "pareggia"; line 12—"rovina" for "ruina"; line 13—"Poiché tant'alto sei, mori contento."

   The sonnet makes reference to the myth of Icarus, the son of Dedalus, who, flying with the waxen wings made for him by his father, drew too close to the sun. The wax melted, and Icarus fell to his death in the Aegean Sea; the sea is also known as the Icarian Sea after him. In his *Secondo libro de madrigali a sei voci,* Striggio included a setting of Tansillo's *Amor m'impenna l'ale e tanto in alto,* itself a poetical elaboration of the present text.

Music
   MS Version—(1) UtrR Lerma, fols. 152v–54r.

[14] S'ogni mio ben havete

S'ogni mio ben havete
Raccolto in le rosate vostre labbia,
Perché tal'hor a me non le porgete?
È pur giusto ch'anch'io
Almen ricuopr'il mio.

(If you have gathered all my love
On your rosy lips,
Why do you not proffer them to me sometimes?
Surely it is right that I, too,
Recover what is mine at least.)

Critical Commentary

Text
   Madrigal. Author unidentified.

Music
   MS Versions—(1) MilBC Tarasconi, fols. 180/190 (no. 197). (2) UtrR Lerma, fols. 154v–55r. (3) (?) LegT 31, p. 95.

Printed Arrangements—(1) Vincenzo Galilei, *Fronimo dialogo . . . nel quale si contengono le vere et necessarie regole del intavolare la musica nel liuto* (Venice: Girolamo Scotto, 1568), No. 88, p. 152. (2) Paolo Virchi, *Il primo libro di tabolatura di citthara . . .* (Venice: Heredi di Girolamo Scotto, 1574), No. 9, p. 18; RISM 1574[14]. (3) Lodovico Agostino, *Il nuovo echo a cinque voci* (Ferrara: Vittorio Baldini, 1583), p. 11. "Fantasia da sonar con gli istrumenti. Ad imitatione del Sig. Alessandro Striggio." (4) Giovanni Antonio Terzi, *Intavolatura di liutto. . . . Libro primo* (Venice: Riccardo Amadino, 1593), No. 11, p. 28; on pp. 29, 31, two *contraponti . . . sopra S'ogni mio ben.*

[15] Quasi improvisa, desiat'e chiara

Quasi improvisa, desiat'e chiara
Luce che, disgombrand'e nub'e venti,
Fa gir per alto mar liet'e contenti
Legn' e nochier, poi ch'el tempo rischiara,
Vid'io l'amat'e cara
Luce che, serenando il ciel intorno
Co bei raggi, cangiò la notte in giorno,
Ond'a la nave mia, dubbia fra l'onde,
L'aure si dimostrar grat'e seconde.

(Like a sudden, longed-for, bright
Light, which sweeps away clouds and winds
And lets ship and helmsman sail through heavy seas
Happy and contented in the clearer weather,
So did I see the beloved and precious
Light which, shining round the sky
With its lovely beams, changed night into day;
Wherewith the breezes showed themselves kind and
    favorable
To my ship floundering amid the waves.)

Critical Commentary

TEXT
    Madrigal. Author unidentified.

MUSIC
    No MS versions, madrigal anthologies, or arrangements.
    Variants—M. 35, all parts, time-signature is $\phi 3$; similarly, m 79. M. 38, quinto, dot not present. M. 45, quinto, dot not present. M. 79, basso, dot not present.

[16] Fortuna, alata il pié, calva la testa

Fortuna, alata il pié, calva la testa,
Et con un crin davanti si dipinge,
E un vecchio zoppo che con quei si resta
Ch'ella si lasci a dietro, anco si finge,
Per mostrar ch'è fugace et che, se presta
La man quand'huom l'incontra, il crin non stringe;
Ella sen va leggiera più che 'l vento
E 'l zoppo vi riman che 'l pentimento.

(Fortune is portrayed on winged foot, bald-headed,
And with a lock of hair in front,
In the company of an old, lame man,
Whom she abandons, even in pretense,
To show she's fleeting and that, although
She lends a hand when a man encounters her,
    the lock does not hold;
She takes her leave more swiftly than the wind,
And the lame man is left only with regret.)

Critical Commentary

TEXT
    Ottava rima stanza. Author unidentified.

MUSIC
    MS Version—(1) UtrR Lerma, fols. 155v–56r.
    Variants—M. 23, all parts, time-signature is 3; similarly, mm. 67 and 77.

[17] Serenata: L'aria s'oscura e di minute stelle

Owing to the exceptional length of the *Serenata,* the English translation appears after each section (= *parte*) of the Italian text. Quotes from popular songs are given in italics both here and in the underlaid text.

Prima parte
L'aria s'oscura e di minute stelle
Già si dipinge il ciel et in ciascuna
Parte i bei raggi suoi scopre la luna;
Ogni fiera selvaggia il sonno affrena,
Taccion gli augelli e i venti;
Sol'io piangend'e sospirando dico:
*"Chi passa per questa strad'e non sospira,
    beato sé"*—
Ma tu, crudel nemica di pietade,
Più sord'assai ch'un asp'o d'orsa alpestra,
Di me ti ridi, e stand'alla finestra
Mi chiami e poi t'ascondi, ond'io piangendo
Humilemente dico: "O sorte, o Dio,
Dite che v'ho fatt'io,
Che sì contraria sete al voler mio."

(The sky grows dark, and with tiny stars
The heavens are now aglitter, and all around
The moon lets loose her lovely beams;
Sleep overcomes all wild creatures,
The birds and the breezes are still;
Alone, weeping and sighing, I call:
*"Lucky the man who passes by this street
    and doesn't heave a sigh"*—
But you, cruel enemy of mercy,
More insensitive by far than snake or wild bear,
You laugh at me, and, appearing at the window,
Call to me, and then hide away, so that in tears
I humbly say: "O Fate, O God,
Tell me what I've done to you,
To make you so contrary to my desire.")

Seconda parte
Ma tu, per darm'al cor maggior tormento,
Mi dici in voci colme di lamento:
"Deh, non t'affliger tanto, vita mia,
Non sai tu ben ch'io son la Margherita,
Che chi mi dona il cor gli do la vita,
    meschina ohimé."
E poi da l'altra parte,
Usando inganni et arte,
Chiamar ti fai da certa vecchiarella
Ch'in fretta dice: "O Polissena bella,
Tua madre ti dimanda."
E in modo tal col far da me partita
Di fuor mi lasci a lamentarmi forte
Di te, d'amor e di mia acerba sorte.

(But you cause greater pain in my heart
By telling me in sob-filled tones:
"Ah, don't trouble yourself so much, my life,
Don't you know well I'm your Margherita
Whoever gives me his heart, I grant my life,
    wretched, alas, as it is."
And then on the other side,
You have a certain little old lady call you,
She hurriedly says: "O Polissena, my beauty,
Your mother's asking for you."
And using this means to get rid of me,
You abandon me outside to complain loudly
About you, about love, and about my cruel fate.)

Terza parte
Apri homai l'usci', o mia gentil signora,
Né in stato tal non mi lasciar perire,
Mentre pôi dar soccors'al mio languire;
Et s'hora che son tre giorni
    ch'io mi partei di Franza,
Cara speranza, solo per tuo amore,
Non mi lasciar più in doglia qui di fuore;
E se la voglia tua pur si compiace,
Che così i'pera senz'haver mai pace,
Non consentir almeno
Che quella tua vecchiazza dispettosa,
Con voce rantacosa,
Mi dica col fuggirsi dal balcon:
"O che nas, o che nason!"
Ma riprendendo il suo malvaggio ardire,
Mostr'a ciascun ch'alberga 'n questa via
Ch'io sia 'l tuo amante et tu la donna mia.

(Open the door now, my noble lady,
Don't leave me to perish in such a state,
While you can relieve my languor;
And it's three days now
    that I should be leaving for France.
Dear hope, just for your love,
Don't leave me out here to suffer any more.
And if it still pleases your will
That I perish like this without peace of mind,

At least don't allow
That spiteful old hag of yours
To say to me in her hoarse voice
As she flees from the balcony:
"O what a nose, o what a big nose!"
But as a reproof to her wicked boldness,
Show to everyone who lives in this street
That I'm your lover and you're my lady.)

Quarta parte
Ohimé, ch'io spasmo—Apri la porta homai,
Dolce mia pastorella,
E mentre sei de più verd'anni tuoi,
In la stagion novella
Dona homai pace a l'affannato core;
Né por l'affetto a questi spensirati
Che van di notte armati, canticchiando:
"Chi zapparà la melica
    un bel baso havrà da me."
Rispose messer lo zanni:
    "la zapparò ben mi."
Messer lo zanni zappe' la melica:
"Mariola, da un bas'a me!"
    "a te?" "a me, sì!"
"Sangue de mi, mai non ti vidi,
Manco un baso ti promisi."
"No?" "mai de no"; no, no, no de mariola, no.
—Che non volendo compiacerli ogn'hora
Se n'andran sempr'in tuo disnor gridando:
"Che t'haggio fatto, o ladra traditora?"
Però, gentil signora,
Apri la porta homai,
E mentre poi scorgendo il mio dolore
Dona homai pace a l'affannato core.

(Oh, dear, I'm in agony—Open the door now,
My sweet little shepherdess,
And while you have your youth,
In the spring of your life,
Grant some respite at last to a heart in distress.
Don't waste your affections on thoughtless fellows
Who pass at night, armed, humming:
"The man who turns over the millet
    will get a lovely kiss from me."
Master johnny replied:
    "I'll turn it over, I will."
Master johnny turned over the millet:
"Swindling woman, give me a kiss!"
    "to you?" "yes, to me!"
"By my life's blood, I've never seen you before,
Far less promised you a kiss."
"No?" "no, never"; no, no, a swindling woman's no, no.
—So that, if you don't always satisfy them,
They'll take their leave, shouting to shame you all the
    while:
"What've I done to you, you treacherous thief?"
So, noble lady,

Open the door now,
And while you then take note of my suffering,
Grant some respite at last to a heart in distress.)

Critical Commentary

TEXT

Four non-identical stanzas. Author unidentified.

As an extreme form of *poesia per musica* (poetry written specifically for musical setting), the *Serenata* is made up of a variety of elements, like a *quodlibet*. There are a number of popular songs (both texts and tunes), identified and cited by Johannes C. Hol, *Horatio Vecchi's weltliche Werke* (Strasbourg: Heitz, 1934; repr. ed., Baden-Baden: Koerner, 1974), pp. 34–36, and Appendix, pp. 2–3. There is at least one citation of a contemporary madrigal. The opening (lines 1–6) recalls (textually) the initial lines of the Petrarch sonnet *Hor che 'l ciel e la terra e 'l vento tace* (*Canzoniere*, CLXIV). For a somewhat different version of the *Serenata* text, with discussion of the various settings, see Einstein, *The Italian Madrigal*, 2:758–61.

The text of the present edition differs in a few respects from that of the 1565 print. These variants are as follows: *seconda parte*, line 3, "Dhe"; *quarta parte*, line 1, "Oime," line 8, etc., "Melica" (with capital).

In the presentation of the popular song texts, the musical phrase has determined, where necessary, the division of the metrical line. Popular song quotations and their sources are as follows: *Prima parte*, line 7, "*Chi passa per questa strad'* . . ."—earliest (musical) version in Filippo Azzaiolo, *Il primo libro de villotte alla padoana con alcune napolitane a quatro voci intitolate villotte del fiore* . . . (Venice: Antonio Gardano, 1557); see also Knud Jeppesen, *La Frottola* (Copenhagen: Hansen, 1968–70), 2: 214, 3: 129. *Seconda parte*, lines 9–10, "*O Polissena bella. / Tua madre ti dimanda*": cf. texts and melodies in two *centoni*: (1) Lodovico Fogliano, *Fortuna d'un gran tempo* (*Frottole libro nono*, Venice: O. Petrucci, 1509 [RISM 1509^2], fol. 38^v) has "Margariton to padre te domanda"; (2) Anon., *E quando andaratu al monte* (*Messa motteti Ca[n]zonni. . .*, Rome: Nicolo de Judici, 1526, fol. 16) has "Margaritum to mare te domanda." Both songs have melodic contours related to those of Striggio's canto, alto, and quinto; cited in Knud Jeppesen, "An Unknown Pre-madrigalian Music Print in Relation to Other Contemporary Italian Sources," in *Studies in Musicology. Essays in the History, Style, and Bibliography of Music in Memory of Glen Haydon*, ed. James W. Pruett (Chapel Hill, N.C.: University of North Carolina Press, 1969), pp. 9–11. The earliest surviving source that contains the "Margaritum" melody, which is found with several different texts and which Jeppesen (p. 11) relates to "a well-known Gregorian psalm intonation," is Giovanni Ambrosio's book of dances (ca. 1460; MS in Venice, Biblioteca Marciana, MS Ital IV, 1227 [11699]), fols. 20–20v, where the text consists of the word "Margaritum" only. See Knud Jeppesen,

"Ein altvenetianisches Tanzbuch," in *Festschrift Karl Gustav Fellerer zum sechzigsten Geburtstag am 7. Juli 1962* (Regensburg: Bosse, 1962), pp. 251, 260. *Terza parte*, line 4, "*Et s'hora che son tre giorni . . .*": northern Italian provenance. Line 13, "*O che nas . . .*": Filippo Azzaiolo's *Terzo libro delle villotte del fiore alla padoana con alcune napolitane e bergamasche a quatro voci et uno dialogo a otto* (Venice: Antonio Gardano, 1569; RISM 1569^{24}) has a triple-time *bergamasca*, *Chi vuol vegni a Bergam, a Bergam'al merca*, p. 7, which has the refrain "O che nas, o che nas, o che babiu, ved'un poco che minchiu." Of the two parts of this print which survive, tenore and basso, the tenore's melodic outline at the refrain corresponds to that of Striggio's setting at mm. 396–97. *Quarta parte*, line 8ff., "*Chi zapparà la melica . . .*": a type of *mariazi (maritaggio)* dialogue, consisting of a dispute or argument between two lovers; possibly of Paduan origin. See Vittorio Rossi, *Storia della letteratura italiana* (Milan, 1904), 2:197. Line 17, "*Che t'haggio fatto . . .*": southern Italian provenance. In addition, the setting of "Apri la porta homai, Dolce mia pastorella" (*quarta parte*, lines 1–2) is a direct citation of a madrigal by Yvo (Ivo) Barry, with the same title, in *Il primo libro di madrigali de diversi eccellenti autori a misura da breve* (Venice: Antonio Gardane, 1542); RISM 1542^{17}. Yvo's canto, alto, tenore, and basso are equivalent to Striggio's sesto, alto, quinto, and basso, respectively, mm. 457–68. See also *terza parte*, opening; and *quarta parte*, mm. 597–606. A triple-time citation of the same phrase from *Apri la porta homai* had occurred already in Giovanthomaso Cimello's *Libro primo de canti a quatro voci . . .* (Venice: Antonio Gardane, 1548), p. 27, in a *Madriale fatto delle principij delli canti e madriali del primo libro di diversi autori*. Modern editions of both Yvo's and Cimello's compositions are in *The Anthologies of Black-Note Madrigals*, ed. Don Harrán, Corpus Mensurabilis Musicae, 73 (American Institute of Musicology, 1978), vol. 1, pt. 1, pp. 32–34; vol. 1, pt. 2, pp. 231–34, respectively.

MUSIC

No MS versions, madrigal anthologies, or arrangements; but note two other settings of the text. (1) Filippo Duc, *Il primo libro de madrigali a quattro voci con una serenata et un dialogo a otto nel fine* (Venice: Girolamo Scotto, 1570); shows acquaintance with Striggio's setting. (2) Anon., *Villotte mantovane a quattro voci* (Venice: Angelo Gardano, 1583). Einstein, in Emil Vogel and Alfred Einstein, *Bibliothek der gedrückten weltlichen Vocalmusik Italiens . . . mit Nachträgen von Prof. Alfred Einstein* (Hildesheim: Olms, 1962), 2:703, suggests that this bipartite setting is by Striggio. It uses different popular tunes from the present setting.

Variants—M. 59, all parts, time-signature is 3. Mm. 453–56, basso, four measures' rest symbol only faintly visible. M. 501, basso, note 2 omitted. M. 525, all parts, time-signature is $\emptyset3$; similarly, m. 556. M. 535, sesto, alto, quinto, basso, no dots present. M. 565, all parts, time-signature is 3.

[18] Rosa eterna, immortal sacro giacinto

Prima parte
Rosa eterna, immortal sacro giacinto
Ch'il crin felice al mio signor cingete,
Dite s'ancor nel secol nostr'havete
Sì nobil crin sì degnamente cinto;

L'antico honor che de i Trevolti ha spinto
La fama ovunque il sol arder vedete
Lampeggi'hor ne la front'alm'ove siete
Tra le virtù l'un fior con l'altro avvinto.

Seconda parte
Er'a tanti minor merti l'alloro,
Et picciol don di quel c'hor l'incorona
Il gran pastor del sempiterno choro;

Et n'è ben degno; anzi, nel ciel risuona
Ch'al crin d'argento ergan le parche d'oro
Altre rose, altri gigli, altra corona.

(Eternal rose, immortal sacred hyacinth
Which wreathe the favored locks of my lord,
Say if you have, as yet, in our century
Wreathed such noble locks so honorably;

The ancient glory, which has borne the renown
Of the Trivulzi to wherever you see the sun blaze,
Now gleams on his beloved brow; there you are
Bound among the virtues, one flower with another.

The laurel was meant for lesser merits,
And was a humble reward compared to that with
which
The great shepherd of the eternal choir now crowns
him;

And he is well worthy of it; indeed, the fact resounds
in heaven
That, in place of the silver wreath, the Fates raise up,
in gold,
Other roses, other lilies, another crown.)

Critical Commentary

Text
Sonnet. Author unidentified.
The poem commemorates Cardinal Antonio Trivulzio (i.e., "Trevolti," line 5; the Trivulzi were an ancient noble family of Milan), papal legate in Paris for the signing of the Treaty of Cateau-Cambrésis (1559); he died suddenly near Paris, on 26 June 1559, on his way back to Italy. See *Biografia universale antica e moderna . . . opera affatto nuova compilata in Francia da una società di dotti* (Venice: Missiaglia, 1829), vol. 58; see also Pompeo Litta et al., *Delle famiglie celebri italiane*, vol. 5 (Milan: Giusti, ca. 1821).

Music
The composer is Alessandro Striggio. No MS versions, madrigal anthologies, or arrangements; excluded from the prints of 1579, 1585, and 1592.

Variants—M. 71, canto, whole-rest omitted. M. 85, quinto, dot missing on note. M. 162, all parts, time-signature is ∅3.

[19] L'alma mia fiamma, oltra le belle bella

L'alma mia fiamma, oltra le belle bella,
C'hebbe qui 'l ciel sì amico e sì cortese,
Anzi tempo per me nel suo paese
È ritornata et a par di sua stella.

Hor comincio a svegliarmi, e veggio ch'ella
Per lo miglior al mio desir contese,
E quelle voglie giovenili accese
Temprò con una vista dolc'e fella.

(My beloved flame, fairer than the fair,
Who enjoyed here a fortune so kind and favorable,
Has gone back, too soon for me,
To her homeland, as equal to her star.

Now I am beginning to rouse myself, and I realize that
she
Was opposed to my desire for the best of reasons,
And tempered those violent, youthful longings
With an air that was sometimes kindly, sometimes
stern.)

Critical Commentary

Text
Sonnet octave. Francesco Petrarca, *Canzoniere*, CCLXXXIX.
Line 4—"È ritornata et a la par sua stella" in *Canzoniere*.

Music
The composer is Claudio da Correggio (= Claudio Merulo). This was the first published madrigal of Merulo. It was not printed elsewhere and was excluded from the Striggio prints of 1579, 1585, and 1592. No MS versions, madrigal anthology prints, or arrangements.

[20] Anchor che col partire

Anchor che col partire
Io mi sento morire,
Partir vorrei ogn'hor, ogni momento,
Tant'è 'l piacer ch'io sento
De la vita ch'acquisto nel ritorno;
E così mill'e mille volte il giorno
Partir da voi vorrei,
Tanto son dolci gli ritorni miei.

(Although on parting
I feel I am dying,
I would wish to leave every hour, every moment,
Such is the pleasure I feel
In the life I gain when I return;

And so a thousand thousand times a day
I would wish to part from you,
So lovely is it when I return.)

Critical Commentary

Text

Madrigal. Attributed to Alfonso D'Avalos, marchese di Vasto: specifically in *Di Giovanthom. Cimello libro primo de canti a quatro voci . . .* (Venice: Antonio Gardane, 1548), p. 2. But this text, "Anchor che la partita," differs considerably from Cambio's, and also, therefore, from that of Rore's famous setting, which first appeared in Cambio's *Primo libro di madrigali a quatro voci* (Venice: Antonio Gardane, 1547; RISM 1547[14]).

Music

The composer is Perissone Cambio (ca. 1520–late 1560s). This madrigal does not appear in any individual print of Cambio's, nor is it printed in later anthologies. It is, however, probably the setting of "Anchor che col partire" included among other madrigals by Striggio that are also in the present collection, in the unexamined RegB 775, No. 23. Cambio's piece was excluded from the Striggio prints of 1566 (Girolamo Scotto), 1579, 1585, and 1592.

Variants—M. 61, alto, redundant quarter-rest. M. 74, sesto, note 1 is d. M. 81, all parts, time signature is ₵3; canto, note 2 has dot in 1560 and in 1565.

CANTO
DI ALESSANDRO STRIGGIO
GENTIL'HVOMO MANTOVANO SERVITORE

dell'Illuftriss. & Eccellentiss. Cofmo de Medici Duca di Firenze, è di Siena. Il primo libro de

Madrigali a fei uoci Nouamente per antonio Gardano con noua gionta Riftampato.

A SEI   VOCI

In Venetia Appreffo di
Antonio Gardano.
1 5 6 5.

Plate I. Alessandro Striggio, *Il primo libro de madrigali a sei voci* (1565 print).
Title page of canto partbook. Actual size: 15.5 × 21.5 cm.
(Courtesy Civico Museo Bibliografico Musicale, Bologna)

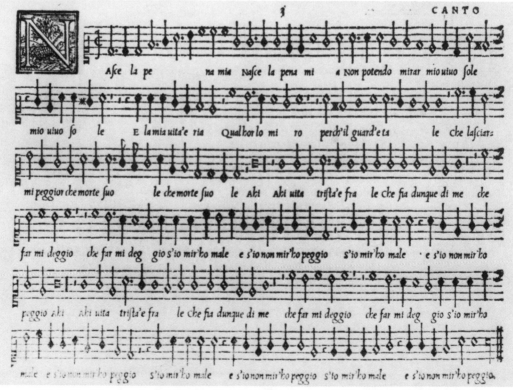

Plate II. Alessandro Striggio, *Il primo libro de madrigali a sei voci* (1565 print).
Nasce la pena mia (No. [2]); canto part, p. 3. Actual size: 15.5 × 21.5 cm.
(Courtesy Civico Museo Bibliografico Musicale, Bologna)

[1] I dolci colli ov'io lasciai me stesso

5

et più m'ap- pres- so, et più m'ap- pres- so.

et più m'ap-pres- so, m'ap- pres- so.

- so,] et più____ m'ap- pres- so, et più m'ap- pres- so.

- so, et più m'ap- pres- so, et più m'ap- pres- so.

- pres- so, et più m'ap- pres- so, et più m'ap-pres- so.

più m'ap-pres- so,] et più m'ap- pres- so.

Seconda parte

Et qual cer- - vo fe- ri- to di sa- et- - ta, fe- ri- to di sa- et- ta____

Et____ qual cer- vo fe- ri- to di sa- et- ta,

Et qual cer-

Et qual cer- - vo____ fe- ri- to di sa- et- ta,

Et qual cer- vo fe- ri- to di sa- et- ta____

12

[2] Nasce la pena mia

16

[3] Anchor ch'io possa dire

22

[4] Lasciat'hai, Morte, senza sol il mondo

Petrarca

Seconda parte

gem-m'a- nel- lo, Sen- - za fior pra- to, o sen- za

sen- za gem-m'a- nel- lo, Sen- za fior pra- to,

o sen- za gem-m'a- nel- lo, Sen- za fior pra-

- nel- lo, o sen- za gem-m'a- nel- lo,

- lo, o sen- za gem-m'a- nel- lo, Sen- za

- to, o sen- za gem-m'a- nel- lo, Sen- za fior pra-

gem-m'a- nel- lo. Non la co-

o sen- za gem-m'a-nel- lo. Non la co- nob-be il mon-

- to,_____ o sen- za gem-m'a- nel- lo. Non

[o sen- za gem-m'a- nel- lo.] Non la co- nob-be il mon- do,

fior pra- to, o sen- za gem- m'a- nel- lo._____

- to, o sen- za gem-m'a- nel- - lo.

E'l ciel, che del mio pian- - - -ri- ma- si, E'l ciel, che del mio

E'l ciel, che del mio

pian- ger qui ri- ma- - si, E'l ciel, che

pian- ger qui ri- ma- si, E'l ciel, che

pian- ger qui ri- ma- si,

-t'hor si fa bel- lo, E'l ciel, che del mio pian-

pian- t'hor si fa bel- lo, E'l ciel, che del mio

pian-t'hor si fa bel- -lo, E'l ciel, che

del mio pian-t'hor si fa bel- lo, E'l ciel, che

del mio pian-t'hor si fa bel- lo, E'l ciel, che del mio pian-

E'l ciel, che del mio pian-

38

[5] Madonna, poich'occidermi volete

42

[6] Se ben di sette stell'ardent'e belle

Bernardo Tasso

con la va- ga fi- glia di____ La- to- na, Pur t'ac- ce- se- r'il cor l'em-

fi- glia di____ La- to- na, Pur t'ac- ce- se- r'il cor l'em-

fi- glia di____ La- to- na, Pur t'ac- ce- se- r'il cor l'em-

fi- glia di ____ La- to- na,

fi- glia di____ La- to- na, di La- to- na,

fi- glia di____ La- to- na, Pur t'ac- ce- se- r'il cor l'em-

- pie fa- cel- le Del fier ar- cier di

- pie fa- cel- le _____

- pie____ fa- cel- le Del fier ar- cier, Del

Del fier ar- cier di Gni- do,

Del fier ar- cier, Del____

- pie____ fa- cel- le Del

Seconda parte

52

[7] Quando vede 'l pastor calar i raggi

56

58

[8] Voglia mi sprona, Amor mi guid'e scorge

68

[9] Là ver l'aurora che sì dolce l'aura

- si, Sì dol- ce- men- te i__ pen-sier

- si,

Sì_____ dol- ce- men- te i__ pen-sier

Sì_____ dol- ce- -men- te i__ pen-sier

- si, Sì dol- -ce- men- te i__ pen-sier

- si,

den-tr'a l'al- ma Mo- -ver mi sen- to a__ chi gl'ha_ tut- t'in

Mo- -ver mi sen- to a chi gl'ha tut-t'in for-

den-tr'a l'al- ma Mo- ver mi sen- -to a chi gl'ha tut-

den-tr'a l'al- ma Mo- -ver mi sen- to a chi gl'ha tut- t'in

den-tr'a l'al- ma Mo- ver mi sen- to a chi gl'ha tut- t'in

Mo- ver mi sen- to a chi__ gl'ha tut- -t'in for-

76

[10] Che fai? che pensi? che pur dietro guardi

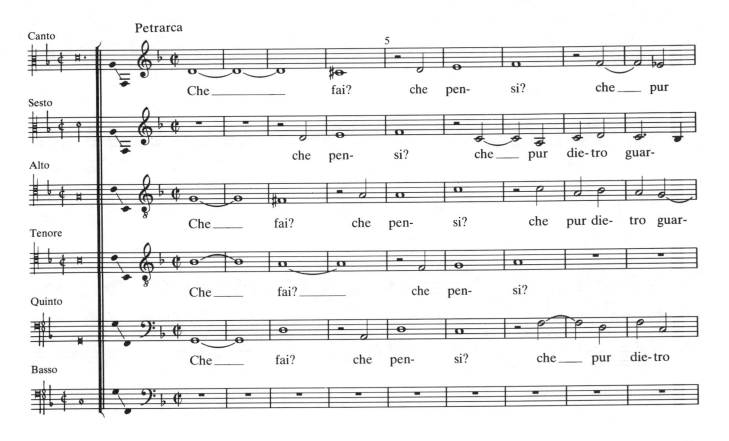

78

[11] Amor, io fallo, e veggio 'l mio fallire

Petrarca

[12] O messagi del cor, sospiri ardenti

Ariosto

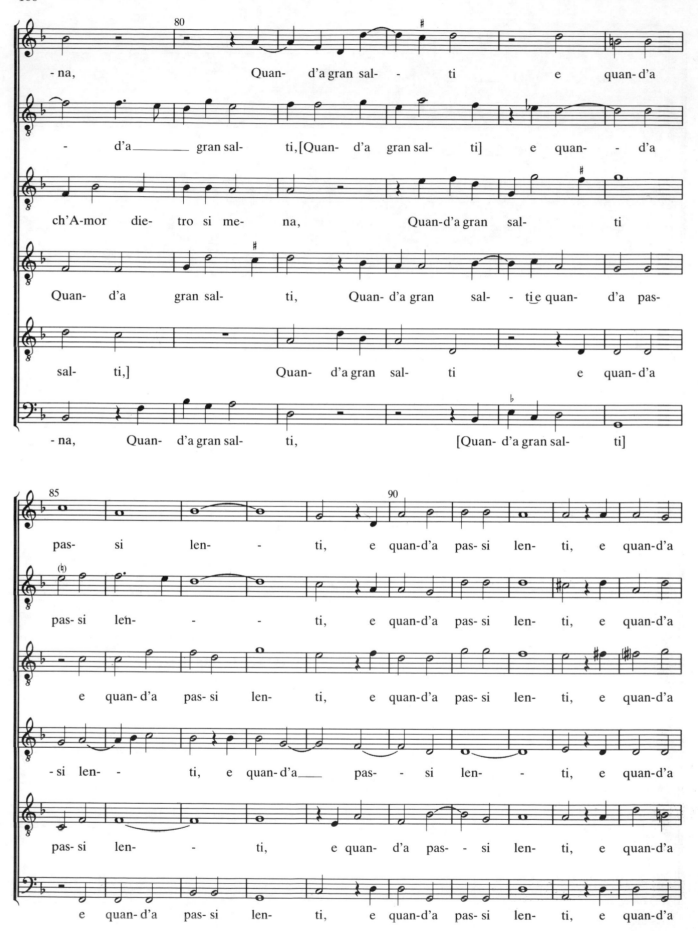

Seconda parte

106

[13] Poi che spiegat'ho l'ale al bel desio

qual vi- ta pa- reg- gia il mo- rir mi- o?

-reg- gia il mo- rir mi- o, il mo-rir mi- o?

il mo- rir mi- o, il mo-rir mi- o?

-ta pa-reg-gia'l mo- rir mi- o, il mo- rir mi- o?

-rir mi- o, il mo- rir mi- o?

mo- rir mi- o, _____ il mo- rir mi- o?

Seconda parte

La vo- ce del mio cor per l'a- ria sen-

La vo- ce del mio

La vo- ce del mio cor per

La vo- ce del mio cor per l'a-ria sen- to:

La vo- ce del mio cor per l'a-ria sen- to, La vo- ce del mio

La vo- ce del mio

-to,   per l'a-ria sen-   to:

cor   per   l'a-   ria   sen-   to: O- ve mi por- ti, te- me- ra-

l'a-ria sen-   to: O- ve mi por- ti, te-   -me-ra-

O-   ve   mi por- ti, te-me- ra-   rio?

cor   per   l'a-ria sen-   -   to: O- ve mi   por-   ti, te-me-ra-

cor   per   l'a-   ria   sen-   to:

-rio?   chi-   -na,   Ché ra- r'è sen- za duol trop-

-rio? chi-   na,   chi-   na,   Ché ra- r'è sen- za   duol trop- p'ar- -di-

chi- na, chi-   na,   Ché ra- r'è sen- za duol trop- - p'ar- -di-

-rio? chi-   na,   chi-   na, Ché ra- r'è sen- za duol trop- -   p'ar- di-

[14] S'ogni mio ben havete

120

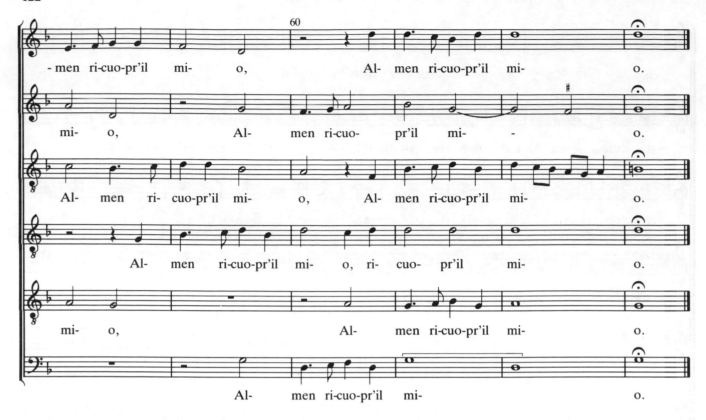

[15] Quasi improvisa, desiat'e chiara

124

128

130

[16] Fortuna, alata il pié, calva la testa

Et con un crin da- van- ti si di-pin- ge, E un

-pin- ge, Et con un crin da- van- ti si _____ di- pin- ge, E un

- ge, Et con un crin da- van- ti si di-pin- ge, E un

- van- ti, Et con un crin da- van- ti si di-pin- ge, E un

- ge, si di- pin- ge, E un

- ge, Et con un crin da- van- ti si di-pin- ge, E un

vec- chio zop- po che con quei si re- sta Ch'el- la si la-scia die- tro,

vec- chio zop- po che con quei si re- sta Ch'el-

vec- chio zop- po che con quei si re- sta Ch'el- la si la-scia

vec- chio zop- po che con quei si re- staCh'el- la si la-scia die- tro,

vec- chio zop- po che con quei si re- staCh'el- la si la- scia die- tro,

vec- chio zop- po che con quei si re- sta Ch'el- la si la-scia

Per mo-strar ch'è fu- ga- ce et che, se pre- sta La

- ce et che, se pre- sta La

ch'è fu- ga- ce] et che, se pre- sta La

Per mo-strar ch'è fu- ga- ce et che, se pre- sta La

Per mo-strar ch'è fu- ga- ce et che, se pre- sta

- ga- ce et che, se pre- sta La

man quan- d'huom l'in- con- tra, il crin non strin- ge;

man quan- d'huom l'in- con- tra, il crin non strin- ge;

man, La man quan- d'huom l'in- con- tra, il crin non strin- ge; El-

man quan- d'huom l'in- con- tra, il crin non strin- ge;

La man quan- -d'huom l'in- con- tra, il crin non strin- ge;

man quan- d'huom l'in- con- tra, il crin non strin- ge;

136

[17] SERENATA: L'aria s'oscura e di minute stelle

*Sesto: "L'aria s'oscura" (prima parte) tacet. "Ma tu, per darmi" (seconda parte) tacet.

140

144

Seconda parte a 5

Ma tu, per dar-m'al cor mag- gior tor- men- to, Mi di-ci in vo- ci

Ma tu, per dar- m'al cor mag- gior tor- men-to, Mi di-ci in vo- ci col- me

Ma tu, per dar-m'al cor mag- gior tor- men- to, Mi di-ci in vo- ci col- me

Ma tu, per dar-m'al cor mag- gior tor- men- to, Mi di-ci in vo- ci col- me

Ma tu, Mi di-ci in vo- ci col- me

col- me di la- men- to: "Deh, non t'af- fli- ger tan- to, vi-

di la- men- to: "Deh, non t'af- fli- ger tan- to,

di la-men- to: "Deh,_____ non____ t'af- fli- ger tan- to, vi-

di la-men-to: "Deh,_____ non____ t'af- fli- ger tan- to, vi-

di la- men- to: "Deh, non t'af- fli- ger tan- to,

- - ta_____ mi- a, *Non sai tu ben ch'io son la Mar-*

vi- - ta mi- a, *Non sai tu ben ch'io son la Mar-*

-ta mi- a, vi- ta mi- a, *Non sai tu ben ch'io son la Mar-*

-ta mi- a, *Non sai tu ben ch'io son la Mar-*

vi- - ta mi- a, *Non sai tu ben ch'io son la Mar-*

Terza parte a 6

Canto: A- pri, A- - pri ho- - mai l'u- sci'o mia gen-

Sesto: A- pri, A- - pri ho- mai

Alto: A- pri, A- - pri ho- - mai___ l'u- sci'o mia___ gen- til si-

Quinto: A- - pri, A- pri ho-mai

Tenore: A- - pri, A- pri ho-mai l'u- - scio A- - pri,

Basso: A-

-til si- gno- - - - ra, Né in

l'u- - sci'o___ mia gen- til si- gno- - - ra, Né in

- gno- - ra, o mia gen- til si- gno- - ra, Né in

l'u- - sci'o mia gen- til___ si- gno- - ra, Né in

A- pri ho-mai l'u- sci'o mia gen- til si- gno- - ra, Né in

- pri, A- - pri ho- - mai l'u-sci'o mia gen- til si- gno- - ra, Né in

164

168

MADRIGALI AGGIUNTI

[18] Rosa eterna, immortal sacro giacinto

che dei Tre- vol- ti ha spin- to

-ti- co ho- nor] che dei Tre-

che dei Tre- vol- ti ha spin- to La

- co ho- nor che dei Tre- vol- ti ha spin- to

-ti- - co ho- nor che dei Tre- vol-

- co ho- nor che dei Tre- vol- ti ha spin- to La

La fa- - ma

-vol- ti ha spin- to La fa- ma

fa- ma o- vun- que il sol ar- -der ve- de-

La fa- - ma o- vun- que il sol ar- -der ve- de-

- ti ha spin- to La fa- ma

fa- ma o- vun- que il sol ar- der ve- te

178

Seconda parte

E- r'a tan- ti mi- nor mer- ti_____ l'al- lo - ro,

E- r'a tan- ti mi- nor mer- ti

E- r'a tan- ti mi- nor mer- ti l'al- lo-

E- r'a tan- ti mi-

E-

E- r'a tan- ti mi- nor mer- ti l'al- lo -

l'al- lo - - ro,

- ro, E- r'a tan- ti mi- nor mer- ti l'al- lo-

- nor mer- ti l'al- lo- ro, E- r'a tan- ti mi- nor mer- ti

- r'a tan- ti mi- nor mer- ti l'al- lo- ro,_____

E- r'a tan- ti mi- nor mer- ti l'al- lo-

184

[19] L'alma mia fiamma, oltra le belle bella

Claudio da Coreggio [=Claudio Merulo]

194

[20] Anchor che col partire

Perissone Cambio